AF564495

# TEACHING AND RESEARCH IN ECONOMICS

# TEACHING AND RESEARCH IN ECONOMICS

*Edited by*

**ANIL KUMAR THAKUR**

*and*

**S.S. SOMRA**

Published on behalf of
THE INDIAN ECONOMIC ASSOCIATION

**DEEP & DEEP PUBLICATIONS PVT. LTD.**
F-159, RAJOURI GARDEN, NEW DELHI-110027

TEACHING AND RESEARCH IN ECONOMICS

ISBN 978-81-8450-361-6



Typeset by S.S. COMPOSERS
3190, Mohindra Park, Shakur Basti, Delhi-110034.

Printed in India at MAYUR ENTERPRISES
WZ Plot No. 3, Gujjar Market, Tihar Village, New Delhi-110018.

Published by DEEP & DEEP PUBLICATIONS PVT. LTD.
F-159, Rajouri Garden, New Delhi-110027.
Phones: 25435369, 25440916
E-mail: ddpbooks@yahoo.co.in • ddpubs@gmail.com
*Showroom:*
2/13, Ansari Road, Daryaganj, New Delhi-110002 • Telefax: 23245122

# Contents

# Preface

Just, we came across with an interesting preface line used by Amartya Sen 'reading makes a full man' according to Francis Bacon, and 'conference a ready man'. Those who missed the $92^{nd}$ Indian Economic Association (IEA) Conference, inaugurated by Prime Minister, Dr. Man Mohan Singh (well known Economist, past President and Life Member of IEA), held at Bhubaneshwar (Orissa) in 2009, may no longer have the chance of being 'ready', but these proceedings offer them an opportunity of reading the papers presented there, and thus achieving 'fullness'.

The Indian Economic Association (IEA) in its $93^{rd}$ year of academic activities, publishing theme-wise edited volumes out of papers contributed to IEA annual conference 2009. As a result of IEA sustained efforts the present volume is prepared as per the conference theme of teaching and research in economics. No doubt the grace of this theme has been increased automatically due to Prof. K.L. Krishana, who has sincerely dedicated his whole life for this profession, chaired the theme session. Dr. S.S. Somra worked as rapporteur in this theme session. This volume contains altogether thirteen papers. The major contributions of these papers are available in a summarised form in the introduction.

We are thankful to President, IEA (2009), Prof. C.H. Hanumantha Rao who provided the opportunity to edit the volume. We also thank all the contributors of this volume without whose cooperation this volume could not be published. We hope this would be helpful to know the theme at a glance. Last, but not least, our thanks to Deep and Deep Publications Pvt. Ltd., New Delhi, for the cooperation and help for excellent publication of the book.

ANIL KUMAR THAKUR
S.S. SOMRA

# List of Contributors

**A.P. Tiwari**, Reader, Department of Economics, Vidyant Hindu College, University of Lucknow, Lucknow.

**Anup K. Mishra**, Lecturer (Economics), DAV PG College, BHU, Varanasi.

**Awadesh Kumar Sinha**, Department of Public Administration, Sir Ganesh Datt College, Patna.

**Bishnu Ray**, Department of L.S.W., A.S. College, Deoghar.

**Biswajit Chatterjee**, Professor of Economics, Chair, Planning and Development Unit and Dean, Faculty of Arts, Jadavpur University.

**Gangadhar V. Kayande Patil**, Reader, BYK College of Commerce, Nashik-422 001(MS).

**M. Mishra**, Reader, Department of Economics, Faculty of Social Science, Banaras Hindu University,Varanasi, UP.

**N.C. Jha**, Reader and Head, Department of Economics, Madhupur College, Madhupur, S.K.M. University, Dumka, Jharkhand.

**N.C. Sahu**, Professor of Economics, Department of Economics, Berhampur University, Bjanja Bihar, Berhampur, Orissa.

**P.K. Sen**, Reader (Economics), DAV PG College, BHU, Varanasi.

**R. Meenakshi**, Reader, Department of Economics, Sri Sarada College for Women, Salem, Tamil Nadu.

**Raj Kishor Pandey**, Project Fellow, DAV PG College, BHU, Varanasi.

**Rakesh S. Patil**, Assistant Professor, Ashoka Institute of Management and Technology, Nashik-422 009 (MS).

**Rekha Jagannath**, Maharani Lakshmi Ammanni Centre for Social Science Research, Bangalore - 560012.

**S.K.L. Das**, Reader and Head, Department of Economics, P.K.R.M. College, Dhanbad.

**Sharmishtha Priti**, Department of Economics, Dr. J. Mishra College, Muzaffarpur.

**T.C.A. Anant**, Professor of Economics, Chair, Planning and Development Unit and Dean, Faculty of Arts, Jadavpur University.

**U.N. Choubey**, Reader in Economics, M.G. Kashi Vidyapeeth, Varanasi.

**V. Krishna Murthy**, Professor in Education, 3/5, Siripuram Quarters, Andhra University, Visakhapatnam, A.P.

**V. Loganathan**, Emeritus Professor of Economics, Sir Theagaraya College, Chennai.

# Introduction

There are thirteen papers in this volume. Collectively they cover a wide range of recent issues and discusses diverse aspects related to teaching and research in economics. In particular, the book contains studies on environmental economics, professional excellence and economics of defence, their relevance and challenges in India under the changing scenario of the world. The book brings a unique ringside perspective to the current issues of teaching and research in economics.

It is a well known fact that the Economics is the queen of Social Sciences and it is often called economic science. No doubt it is called a soft science, relative to hard sciences such as physics, chemistry, and biology. It is admitted that one cannot ignore the interdependence of the observer and the observed in any branch of discipline. As a result, there is some element of subjectivism that enters into subjects. But in order to minimize the damage that subjectivism can cause to a scientific discipline one must always keep in mind objectivism by posing the questions: "Do you see what I see? Do others, within our profession and outside our profession, see what you and I see, or do they see something different? Have I explained everything so that others can replicate my study and or experiment and verify my results? Have I ruled out convincingly other possible alternative explanations of data by giving each one of them sufficient chance?" As long as we keep these issues of objectivity in mind, it is acceptable to subjectively and aggressively intervene, i.e. create a deliberate observer-observed interaction, to hasten the process of making economics more qualitative and scientific than what it is today and save the discipline from the onslaught on its lack of scientificness from its critics within and outside the discipline.

The compartmentalisation of economics into mathematical

economics, statistical methods, computational methods, and experimental economics, without due integration and a proper balance in all may create the crisis. We take this opportunity to emphasize that we need to make experimental economics a major tool to make economics more scientific and relevant. There can be few areas of research in experimental economics that address resource allocation problems that experimental economics and economics could receive wider acceptance from the developing countries.

The first paper by T.C.A. Anant deals with about the broad contours of recent changes in teaching and research in economics. He wrote the present year marks two anniversaries. Twenty years ago, the UGC's Curriculum Development Committee (CDC) submitted a report on modernizing the teaching in economics, and almost forty years ago, the Government of India had established the ICSSR to strengthen research capacity in the social sciences. He tries to review some of the developments since these two landmarks events in the teaching and research and examine their implications for the discipline in India. He put stress on bifurcation into undergraduate and postgraduate curricula. In undergraduate, the pass-course curriculum is aimed at students who seek a liberal arts degree, and is also often used for providing subsidiary courses in other honours curricula. The honours curricula on the other hand are viewed as the first step in the training of the professional economist. The postgraduate training in economics which is more focused on training students to develop formal models. The research process can be seen in terms of its role in quality assurance, training and disciplinary evolution. The issue of research quality assurance, this is done in academia through the role played by disciplines in insuring methodological correctness, and through peer review conducted through the non-anonymous processes of journals on the other. This process of peer review takes place in a healthy system through the internal processes of developments, and institutes, associations and journals and other vehicles of scholarly communications. Social science research in general and economics in particular, has traditionally been pulled between the competing drivers of a curiosity about the functioning of society in all its diverse dimensions and the practical needs of policy-makers and managers in government, civil society and the private sector for reliable information and professional analysis.

In his paper Biswajit Chatterjee stresses on the importance of taking a new look at the problems of teaching economics in our country on all fronts: what to teach, how to teach and how to evaluate. The problems are not simple, yet not insurmountable. If our profession has to rise to the needs of changing environment and produce economist of high quality and originally, a fundamental change from what it is now appears essential. He mentioned the main problem of teaching of economics in India is the vast diversity in quality, which is due to several factors including availability of good quality teachers. The student population also has wide variety of background as a result of which we are handicapped of penetration of analytical modern methods to be taught.

The paper by M. Mishra and N.C. Sahu suggest the growing role of environment economics. In the paper they have explained the people all over the world have realised that environment is not just the study of various flora and fauna , but a synthesis of study of various branches of knowledge like science, economics, philosophy, ethics, anthropology, etc. Therefore, a study of environmental economics calls for a detailed understanding about various environmental factors, their influences in the economy, their functions upon the environment, and their impact upon the life of people of the present and future.

Next, the paper by Rekha Jagannath discusses research in economics in Indian colleges. It reflects that over the decades after globalisation, provisions for college teachers to conduct research have better hopes. Particularly the $11^{th}$ plan has tried to make torrential change in the college education structure and so as to enable research amidst the other changes. Previous restrictions are largely relaxed. She also suggests that the discriminations between pure sciences and social sciences should be removed with respect to research grants allocation.

The paper by R. Meenakshi focuses on professional excellence in economics, of course there has to be someone among them to provide the lead. She explains very well the professional excellence, pattern, activities and need of quality and skill in research.

V. Krishna Murthy's paper highlights how the training in economics for the M.Phil. and Ph.D. programmes is important. He explains our present economic ailments are those associated with or arising directly from the problems of economic growth. It is highly important that the Indian scholars of M.Phil. and Ph.D. degrees understand and appreciate these problems and undertake studies to identify the variables involves in the process of economic growth and offer suggestions to remove the bottlenecks and achieve sustainable economic development.

Next we have a joint paper by Anup K. Mishra, P.K. Sen and Raj Kishor Pandey on global and quality education: how can this be ensured? He highlights the various issues of impact of globalisation on employment, information technology, the social implications, etc. in changing scenario of the world.

The paper by Gangadhar V. Kayande Patil and Rakesh S. Patil focuses on a comparative study of teaching and research in economics and other courses. They have put stresses on promotion and research and teaching status of a teacher, actual and preferred uses of time, etc. in a comparative mode of teaching and research.

S.K.L. Das and Bishnu Ray discusses Education in New-Socio-Economic Order and shows that the course structure in U.G. and P.G. level should be redesigned which will suit the changing conditions. For skill development of our students there is need of developmental workshops, annual conferences and seminars. These should be made compulsory in the departments where financial and infrastructural facilities are provided. Besides the classroom interactions, a case study analysis and for practical exposures for each student through campus industry interactions should be incorporated into the syllabus. Case study should be made compulsory element of the subject.

N.C. Jha and Awadesh Kumar Sinha pointed out that teaching in economics at undergraduate level colleges in rural areas a great challenge. They pointed out various problems associated with regard to enrolment, course of study, quality of students, effectiveness of teaching process viewed from student-teacher ratio and per teacher lecture or contact periods per week, work load of teachers faced by the rural and semi-urban colleges. They also suggest improving the quality in research and teaching. There is need to increase the number of teachers in proportion to increase in the number of seats in the courses for maintaining optimal ratio.

The paper by U.N. Choubey and Sharmishta Priti focuses

on the forthcoming challenges in the profession. They have explained that constant evaluation is required to provide desired level of teaching, talented and skilled manpower and quality research with innovations and experimentations.

V. Loganathan discusses the problems of teaching in economics. He suggests that the teaching in economics should be practical according to the country requirements. According to him, there are two types of school of thoughts in our country, one is influenced by the western vision and another is by endogenous customs of the country. Finally, he concluded by saying that the task facing the economist in India is not so much of rejecting the irrelevant as of constricting the relevant.

A.P. Tiwari discusses the economics of defence and its relevance in economics. He explained the application of economics to national defence is a relatively new branch of discipline but put the issue as a part of the syllabus of the economics. He shows various points through them so that we can increase the effectiveness of the topic in economics.

Almost all the papers have explained concern about the improvement in the quality of teaching and research in economics under the changed scenario of the world. No doubt collectively these have suggested the various issues to make effective, efficient and improvement in teaching and research in economics. In this way one more last point but not least, I want to mention about the selection process of teachers. The selection process must be fair in the universities as well as in the colleges. Because, if the selection process is manipulated by the higher authority, that would highly be destructive for the system and create the unrest in existing staff and good quality of competent. However, there emerged several issues to improve the quality of teaching and research in economics that could meet the challenges in future: need of placement cells in the universities and colleges; the courses should be designed according to the requirements of the corporate sector or practical applicability of the jobs; work assessment of the research and teaching is necessary to maintain and improve the quality of the research and teaching; and good quality of teachers and training programmes are also necessary to improve the standard of economics from teaching as well as research point of view.

Paper writers were given a very wide choice of topics

dealing with any regulatory measures whether UGC or universities and colleges concerning teaching and research in economics. But the theme appears to put more stress on implementation of policies by different organisations in the education field properly so the quality can be improved in the research and teaching in economics to meet out the forthcoming challenges of the changing scenario of the world.

ANIL KUMAR THAKUR
S.S. SOMRA

# Teaching and Research in Economics

T.C.A. Anant

## INTRODUCTION

This year marks two anniversaries. Twenty years ago, the UGC's curriculum development committee (CDC) submitted a report on modernizing the teaching of economics, and almost 40 years ago, the government of India had established the ICSSR to strengthen research capacity in the social sciences. This paper marks a somewhat idiosyncratic stock taking.

At the outset it is useful to take a brief look at the way economics has evolved as a profession. In the pre-independence period economics research in India could be classified into two main segments. First was the colonial enterprise which included luminaries like Thomas Malthus, James and John Stuart Mill and Jeremy Bentham amongst others. They along with the providing the foundations of modern neo-classical economics also provided the intellectual support to the imperial enterprise in India. This connection continued until much later, with Keynes beginning his career as clerk in the India office and his first book was on Indian Currency and Finance. In contrast to this imperialist tradition, a nationalist response was also evident with writings of Dadabhai

Naoroji, BR Ambedkar, ... and others. This body of work sought to describe the Indian reality and with it the development imperative. It is with this background we see the Indian constitution seeking to secure social and economic justice for all its citizens and explicitly stating in Art. 38 "State to secure a social order for the promotion of welfare of the people. The State shall strive to promote the welfare of the people by securing and protecting as effectively as it may a social order in which justice, social, economic and political, shall inform all the institutions of the national life. Confronting this enormusly raised levels of expectations from the state was a Knowledge gap, of what is the character and components of public policy to be followed. In 1947, The Government of India sought to fill this gap through the establishment of the Planning Commission. But the process of formulating plans needed information and knowledge about specific social problems. This was sought to be filled in two ways. Various ministries set-up research institutes, NCAER, The Agro Economics Research Centers, National Productivity Council and on. In addition in 1953 the Planning Commission established the research programs committee to work out and administer suitable schemes of research and investigaiton into social, economic and administrative problems relating to national development. These initial efforts marked the first attempts to incorporate social science and more specifically economic research into policy formulation. There was another dimension. The end of the Second World War saw the emergence of Soviet Russia as an illustration of the power of state-led and controlled development. The emergence of communist China and eastion Europe appeared as a challenge to the west and the idea of democracy. In this context India was viewed as a novel laboratory for development in a democratic setting and that India's development strategy combinig markets and the state was seen as a counter to the emerging "Threat too in the Indian experience." I have taken this somewhat long digression to partly emphasis why the study of the India reality is intimately linked to the development of the discipline of economics. A fact unfortunately lost sight of in the mainstream teaching and research in Economics.

In my lecture today, I review some of the developments since these two landmarks events in teaching and research and examine their implications for the discipline in India.

## 2. THE ECONOMICS CURRICULUM

The teaching of economics is bifurcated into undergraduate and postgraduate (Masters) curricula. It would be useful to examine these in some detail.

### 2.1 The Undergraduate Curriculum

The Undergraduate curriculum is schizophrenic divided as it is between the what is termed as the pass course, and the honours course. Both of these are typically three years in length. The pass course curriculum is aimed at students who seek a liberal arts degree, and is also often used for providing subsidiary courses in other Honours curricula. The Honours curricula on the other hand is viewed as the first step in the training of the professioinal economist. The distinction may be classified as the difference between "Thinking like an economist *vs.* a liberally educated person who knows economics."

However, if we examine the curricula, in practice, this difference finds little reflection in the content. The curricula for the pass course is a truncated version of what is taught in the Honours program. Thus in the report of the CDC we find that the pass course virtually replicates topics and titles as in the Honours program. This begs the question of what is this curriculum seeking to achive.

If the aim is to provide some insights into the way economists reason, then it is better not to teach a mechanical program of consumer theory, producer theory, etc. But instead develop some key concepts through a more applied discussion. An outline of how this may be done can be seen in the discussion in the proceedings on the 114th annual meeting of the AEA. The logic of this approach would be to consider redesigning the pass course not as a lower level stepping stone to training an economist. But rather as a vehicle to provide literacy about the way economists. This also implies that existing textbooks need to be reevaluated for this purpose. Since most of them are written typically as principles or intermediate level books but essentially targeting people who will eventually become economics majors.

Turning now to the Honours curriculum. This follows more convetional lines. Divided as it is between a core curriculum and an optional curriculum. The core comprises of papers in theory, quantitative methods and Indian economics. This is then supplemented by a vast collection of modules termed optional covering various applied and theoretical areas in economics. The description of core and optional are however somewhat misleading as the choice is very often not at the level of the student, but is at level of the college or university offering the course. The principal concerns here the same as they were twenty years ago, the divorce between the theory and applied sections of the course. This Indian concerns get shelved off into either the Indian Economics course, or as a separate section in the same course. In either case the impression is left that theory is not applicable to Indian contexts. Let me illustrate with an example I use as a question on selection committees. Ask students about examples of public goods you get a range of examples Health care, Education, Power and virtually all state supplied goods services are perceived as suitable examples. When you ask them a more direct question relating to the definition of public goods, you will get a reasonably correct statement. The dissonance occurs because the theory is rarely illustrated with examples the student can relate with[1].

### 2.2 The Postgraduate Curriculum

Turning now to the Postgraduate training in economics which is more focused on training students to develop technical and analytical skills necessary to develop formal medels. This stage continues the undergraduate lack of emphasis on how such models are applied, mechanisms and institutions of policy design. The training at this stage is excessively mechanistic, with differnet models being applied labels and described in stylised boxes: Solow Growth Model, Putty-Models, Neo-Classical nodels and so on. The attempt is more to ensure completion of a designated set of topics rather than as a integrated analytical structure. This form of teaching gets reinforced by the type of questions posed in the JRE-NET exams. The economics paper is in two parts. The first part worth 100 marks has 50 multiple choice questions. In this list 8 questions required examinees to temporally sequence, models, personalities and concepts; another 8 questions sought to link concepts and theories to people; and 4 questions were on facts like India's ranking in the HDI. Thus 40% of the papers had no analytical content. The remaining 60% was based on a few questions with a analytical content and large number of definitions. The second paper has more descriptive answers and is for 200 marks but even here the focus on analytical questions is relatively small. There is very little effort to assess a students ability to apply theory to solve simple problems.

## 2.3 Miscellaneous Issues

### *2.3.1 Regional Languages*

There has been a vast increase in the instruction in regional languages. The difficulty is that in most of these languages there is a near absence of teaching material in the language. Efforts of various government agencies has led to the availability of a bare minimum of text-books, but research papers, reference material, etc. are all in English. Further most quality research is in English. A good example is that some of the best work in India in economics is published in *EPW, Indian Journal of Labour Economics, Indian Journal of Agricultural Economics* and so on, all of them are only available in English. Most government commitee reports are in English. It is only a relatively small set of documents tabled in parliament that are in Hindi as well. The case of other Indian languages is even worse.

### *2.3.2 Training in Research Methodology*

One of the key objectives of Masters training is to motivate and develop students to become professional economists. The limitations of the curriculum as well as the virtual absence of any attempt to teach research methodology. This lack of training manifests itself later in the nature of research proposals. The ICSSR and the UGC have now for over forty years being trying to build up research capacity amongst university and college teachers. However the overall experience with this effort has been poor. In addition to proposals that are weak in setting out the questions of interest, literature of relevance ande methodology, the better proposals essentially amount to what are descriptive efforts. The importance to generalisation and analysis is poorly understood. We will return to this issue after our discussion on the research structure.

### 2.4 Looking Ahead

In closing, it worth turning our attention to some developments after the curriculum committee had submitted its report. The micro-computer revolution had certainly begun before but its subsequent development were both unanticipated and breath-taking. Today at a relatively low cost it is possible for a student or teacher to have access to computer resources earlier available only in major universities and the IITs. The availability of public and share were have made these resources extremely accessible. The second development has been the growth of the Internet. Unfortunately even though these developments have made widespread inroads in the domain of social communications. Their use in teaching is still somewhat limited. The undergraduate and for the most part masters curriculum is largely text driven and there is limited space for student exploration and discovery. The availability to material of interest and relevance for a student of economics on the net is now enormous, a useful place for a person to start is the resources for economists page maintained by the American Economics Association, HTTP://www.aeaweb.org/rfe/, the interested scholar can also discover a variety of other resources in different continents. In India, too, there are valuable resource on the net what is missing however is an index site organizing and providing links of interest to economists. Further what is needed is an effort to demonstrate how these resources may be best used for teaching and research.

## 3. THE RESEARCH STRUCTURE

In the introduction we had noted that at independence, the newly independent country wanting to develop itself had turned to social scientists to advise it on the steps it may take for this purpose. This was done through a variety of means which included creating captive research institutes, and starting a program for sponsored research under the aegis of the planning commission. Unfortunately this effort very early on ran into serious capacity constratains. There was a felt need to examine the research structure with a view to give it a clearer focus and make it more effective. Thus in August 1965 the Planning Commission set-up a committee of social science research under the Chairmanship of Prof. V.K.R.V. Rao (CSSR). This report was accepted and led to the formation of the ICSSR.

### 3.1 The Research Institutions

A decade later in 1979, in a two part article in the *Economic and Political Weekly*, Myron Wiener reviewed the structure of social science research in India and he identified four types of institutions engaged in social science research. These were described as:

1. Government controlled research organisations: These included bodies such as the Registrar General of the Census which are directly controlled by the central government. And others which have the structure of autonomous bodies but are in practice departmental undertakings such as National Institute for Rural Development, V.V. Giri National Labour Institute, National Productivity Council, etc.
2. The second group consisted of functionally autonomous but government funded institutions. This group is dominated by institutes receiving funding from ICSSR, but would include institutions like the Tata Institute for Social Sciences and also would include a number of newer research institutes set-up by government departments and Ministries as autonomous societies.
3. Then we have social science departments of universities and colleges.
4. Finally, we have Private research consultancies that are clubbed with a variety of non-governmental organisations that include research amongst their field of activities.

Wieners classification and assessment remains valid even today. Except that the profile and role of the different elements have changed. In so far as the first group is concerned the lack of autonomy and leadership has dwarfed the potential of these bodies and they remain for the most part data gatherers and conduct the most routine inquiries.

The Committee for social science research had in addition

to its recommendation for setting up an Indian Council of Social Science Research, the ICSSR also suggested that one of the main functions of the Council would be "To give maintenance grants to research institutions in social sciences that do not constitute either affiliated or constituent institutions of statutory universities in India." In response to this recommendation the government and later the ICSSR started entering into dialogues with state governments for establishing new research institutes. The objective was to supplement the university system and help rectify some of the major gaps in social science research in India. This led to the setting up of institutes in Calcutta, and Allahabed. In addition some pre-existing institutes were also brought under the scheme. Ultimately 28 institutes were set-up. Wiener reviewing this process noted that "Which states were given funds to create social science research institutes was determined by whether local scholars or public figures took the initiative to create a center, and whether they had support within the Union Ministry of Education and/or the state government. Some of the initiative came from scholars in public life. Three research centers in South India were initiated by former vice-chancellors and one of these vice-chancellors is the founder of three such institutions. The Minister of Education was particularly sympathetic to proposals from political associates of his in Calcutta and Luchnow, while one public figure associated with the Gandhian movement played an important role in obtaining government support for a research institute in Varanasi. (Wiener, *op. cit.*) The idiosyncratic approach described by Prof. Wiener continued in the eighties, and has had major consequences for the nature of their development. Some of these institutes have emerged as major centers for social science research and have received national and international acclaim for the quality of their work. On the other hand, there are others which were poorly planned have had serious problems in attracting faculty and have also suffered from problems of inadequate leadership. However, the ICSSR review committee notes that the nature of funding of these institutes has meant that they have needed to look for external sponsors for funding and this has been hampered in their ability to do independent researches. The problem is not with doing sponsored research, but rather the fact that there is little incentive to convert these research into academic publications, an issue to which we turn to in greater detail in the next section.

Universities are the oldest locations for research in economics and other social sciences. The first universities were established over 150 years ago and some colleges are even older. However, post-independence the general perception has been that universities have declined in importance because of excessive focus on expanding teaching. In spite of that in a recent study analyzing SCOPUS data from 1996 to 2007 show that the highest rank amongst Indian institutions publishing in social sciences is that of Delhi University with 779 publications and 531 citations and Jawaharlal Nehru University is in fourth place with 377 publications and 195 citations. In fact only the Indian Statistical Institute in second place is the only research institution in the top five. However, this overall picture cannot disguise the fact that both in terms of volume and dispersion the performance of Indian universities is quite in terms of volume and dispersion the performance of Indian universities is quite poor. There are a number of reasons for this poor performance, the teaching burden is only a part, though quite a significant part one may add. The internal structure of universiy administreation in providing and administering research grants; the relatively low value, until recently, attached to academic research.

The weakness of the university system in research administration and the large allocation of public funds for research has led to a huge growth in private research institutes or NGOs. The Report of the Fourth ICSSR Review Committee using data gathered by NASSDOC indicated over 800 such institutes. This does not include a substantial number of essentially post box NGOs operating in different metropolises of the country, as ancillaries to our universities and large research institutes. The difficulty is that there is no understanding of what exactly is a research institutes, and what is its role as distinct from that of a stand alone researcher, Principally a research institution should have spaces for dialogue, through seminars, workshops, and colloquial which act as devices to maintain and promote quality, as well as for training for younger yet to be established scholars. We turn to this issue in our next section.

### 3.2 The Research Process

We now examine some of the consequences of this institutional structure on the research process. This can be seen in terms of its role in quality assurance, training and disciplinary evolution. Turning first to the issue of quality assurance, this is done in academia through the role played by disciplines in ensuring methodological correctness, and through peer review conducted through the non-anonymous processes of journals on the other. This process of peer-review takes place in a healthy system through the internal processes of departments and institutes, associations and journals and other vehicles of scholarly communication. But these too are subject to crisis. In the west central to the notion of disciplines are the academic departments of universities. The strength of those departments in terms of their participation in research has ensured the continued relevance of this facet in academic research in developed countries. Unfortunately, in India, academic departments as we noted have been marginalised in research. They have been supplanted instead by the research institutes and NGOs. The latter by their very structure are not suited for academic quality control. The former are often in their structure sometimes mandated to be inter-disciplinary in character, this raises a separate set of issues which are not often appreciated. In India today there is a tendency to chant multi-disciplinary/inter-disciplinary as if they were a mantra for quality. This misses the point that inter-disciplinary research we have in mind either a cooperation between scholars in two disciplines working on a common issue or a scholar in one discipline analyzing problems developed in another discipline but with the tools from his parent discipline. Both forms of work require a prior training in a basic academic discipline. Economics in particular has over the last century evolved into a formal discipline with a clear methodological foundation. The curiculum development committee recognized this by the primary it gave to the core curricula. In a balanced areas of the core curricula, the combined input of these scholars provides a basis of internal quality control not possible in inter-disciplinary research institute with only a small set of its faculty in economics.

In the area of academic journals as well, there is once again a huge number emanating from associations, university departments, and research institutes. Unfortunately, concepts of peer-review and academic independence of these journals is a function of the strength of the sponsoring institution. Thus given the weaknesses in the sponsoring institute often translates to peer-review systems that are weak and not systematic. In spite of this some Journals have maintained good standards, the *Indian Journal of Labour Economics, Sociological Bulletin, Journal of Quantitative Economics* are some of the notable examples.

In addition, there are some very good journals published by some leading publishing houses which are focused on India. But on the whole, the overall number of such journals is small given the size of the academic community in India. In addition, most Indian journals are not indexed, or listed in major international listing sources. There is no Indian source for indexing or listing, the combined effect of these is that most Indian published work is invisible. In academic structures this is as good as there being no work at all. There has been some recent attempts to give greater visibility to academic work, through participation in REPEC, SSRN, Esocialsciences.org but this is extremely fragmentary and limited to the few well known research institutions and universities.

## 4. THE INTERFACE BETWEEN TEACHING AND RESEARCH: DOCTORAL STUDIES

The training of future researchers has been affected by Higher Education Policy in India; which has been driven largely viewing higher education through a prism of producing skilled manpower for the productive sectors. Ph.D.'s in this world view was seen not so much a component of an effective research process but rather as a "Capital Good" for the production of skilled manpower. Thus production of Ph.D.'s was a task to be allocated to specialised research institutions, as that was more of an adjunct of the policy process. This policy of developing research infrastructure independent of the university system has induced weaknesses in the research training process. The weaknesses of the departments hampered their own production of research students (not in numerical terms but in terms of the quality and relevance of work done by them). This was because the training of young scholars through postgraduate and doctoral programs, by active researchers, provides for future talent and the mechanism for the system to continuously renew and enlarge itself. A second problem arose in the facts that these research institutes were, explicitly by original mandate, not universities;

they needed to get affiliation with universities to design and run Ph.D. programs. Secondly, the research institutes themselves were at least in social sciences structured as inter-disciplinary or multi-disciplinary in character. But the requirements of university affiliation meant that they would prepare students for disciplinary Ph.D.'s. This implied that instead of deveolping new *sui generis* doctoral research programs of their own, they emulated and incorporated the weaknesses of the universities structure of disciplinary programs. The larger research institutes like ISEC, CDS were able to circumvent some of these limitations by virture of the fact that their focus become almost exclusively in economics. Further given their size they were able to get a reasonable coverage of subject areas. They did however remain weak in theory thus compounding the weaknesses in the overall structure of formal analysts.

## 5. CONCLUSION

It is useful at the end to examine the impact of this structural story on the process of disciplinary evolution as well. Social Science Research, in general and Economics in particular, has traditionally been pulled between two competing drivers. These are: (a) a curiosity about the functioning of society in all its diverse dimensions; and (b) the practical needs of policy-makers and managers in government, civil society and the private sector for reliable information and professional analysis. Thus in academia there has been a tension between the cries for "relevance" on one hand and the freedom and ability of an individual scholar to pursue his curiosity on the other. This debate is not unique to India and finds echo in the various social science professions all over the world. The challenge in India is to maintain space for what Prof. Beteille has termed as "delayed return" research in an environment where "relevance" attracts more funds, greater recognition and acclaim or one can put it differently by referring to Keynes "Practical men, who believe themselves to be quite exempt from any intellectual influences are usually the slaves of some defunct economists. Madmen in authority, who hear voices in the air, are distilling their frenzy from some academic scribblers of a few years back. Thus these drivers are not separate but periodically re-enforce each other.

Unfortunately the limitations on public funding and the emphasis on own generation of funds has meant that research establishments and universities have to forcus on the requirements of funding agencies. There is very little effort to sponsor long-term "Pure Research." An imbalance between these different components tends to weaken the basic disciplines of economics in India, and manifests itself with the limited space for 'theorists' in Indian academic establishments.

Research which is not immediately focused or derived from issues of current policy concern often is the basis for future policy. The importance of what is sometimes termed as "irrelevant" or "abstract" researh in developing the future growth of the disciplines should not be understated. One such example can be seen from the field of economics. Game theory for a long time was seen as mathematical curiosity. Today it is used in a wide variety of uses from designing auction mechanisms to understanding political processes and governance systems. The current scenario in addition to its noted limitations is also excessively focused on the needs of current policy. This has meant that major developments in theory still remain a prerogative of the west. Correcting this situation requires that the profession itself learns to take stock and initiate a process of engagement and dialogue with various elements of the state and civil society.

## References


W. Lee Hansen, Michael K. Salemi, and John J. Siegfried, "Use it or Lose It: Teaching Literacy in the Economics Principles Course", *The American Economic Review*, Vol. 92, No. 2, Papers and Proceedings of the One Hundred Fourteenth Annual meetings of the American Economic Association (May, 2002), pp. 463-72.

Robert E. Lucas Jr., Alan B. Krueger, Rebecca M. Blank, "Promoting Economic Literacy: Panel Discussion", *The American Economic Review*, Vol. 92, No. 2, Papers and Proceedings of the One Hundred Fourteenth Annual Meeting of the American Economic Association (May, 2002), pp. 473-77.

David Colander and Kim Marie McGoldrick, "The Economics Major as Part of a Liberal Education", Paper presented at the 2009 AEA Meetings.

Report of the fourth Review Committee of the Indian Council of Social Science Research (ICSSR).

M.R. Goodall, "Planning in India: Research and Administration", *Public Administration Review*, 1957, Vol. 17, No 2.

Planning Commission, Government of India (1968), Report of the Committee on Social Science Research.

Myron, Wiener, "Social Science Research and Public Policy in India", *Economic and Political Weekly*, Vol, 14, No. 37, pp. 1579-87 and *EPW*, Vol. 14, No. 38, pp. 1622-28.

A Comparative Study of Social Science Research in India, China and Brazil", B.M. Gupta, S.M. Dhawan and Ugrasen Singh, NISTADS, 2008.

Gautam Desiraju, "Science Education and Research in India", *EPW*, Vol 43, No. 24, June 14-20, 2008.

Prof. Pushpa Bhargava, "On the organisation of Science Research in India", *EPW*, Vol. 43, No. 31, July 26-Aug 1, 2008.

# Teaching and Research in Economics in India

## An Introspection

Biswajit Chatterjee

About twenty years back, the IEA Trust for Research and Development under the initiative of late Professor Sukhomoy Chakraborty organized a workshop on the same theme and outlined the need for improving the course curriculum and teaching of Economics in Indian Universities. More than half a dozen of stalwarts in the profession who participated in that workshop and gave valuable suggestions are no longer with us in this world, and we are still groping with the same sort of problems as were identified in that workshop almost two decades back. Teaching and research in economics in our country is still largely in problem areas and efforts to improve them through different measures by the UGC has not been successful in general, although there are a few exceptions.

The main problem of teaching of Economics in India is the vast diversity in quality, which is due to several factors including availability of good quality teachers. The student population also has wide variety of backgrounds as a result of which we are handicapped of penetration of analytical modern methods to be taught. Way back in 1950s when students from Indian universities used to visit the advanced centres of learning in the west like the London School of Economics, they were expected to cover at least the Marshall's Principle of Economics, and basic statistical and mathematical techniques like Calculus, and those who did not have that background were forced to abandon higher learning in Economics and switch to related subjects like politics. Similar situation still persists, except that without adequate training in mathematical methods, one would not get admitted to US/European Universities in Economics. The outflow of Indian students to top centres of economics in US and European universities are mainly from selective centres of excellence in economics in the country. Even within India the training of students of economics with adequate exposure to mathematical and quantitative techniques for economics is limited, and this limitation is reflected in the limited quality of researches in economics undertaken in the country.

Teaching a subject that has various dimensions and is continuously changing is a difficult task, and in a country like India, where education is constrained by several socio-economic factors, teaching economics meaningfully and consistently (implying an integration between various elements of education at different stages of training) raises several questions, some of which are methodological and epistemological, some practical and some conceptual. Broadly speaking, the subject involves three sots of questions and three sots of people in academics. The questions are: (a) what to teach; (b) how to teach, and (c) how to evaluate?' The following set of people are involved: (i) students, (ii) teachers, and (iii) researchers. In what follows I shall review various issues associated with teaching of economics in India in general and the problem of teaching some specific branches of economic in particular. I shall be ignoring organisation and management problems as they arise in course of teaching any subject, but not specific to economic teaching. For example, if in a given university or a college (the question of academic autonomy is related to this) we do not have sufficient reading materials or even if we have funds to procure them but they are not available to the consumers, then there is definitely a constraint for teaching what we consider desirables. Sometimes, the colleges do not have freedom to adjust the course contents because the universities prescribed a particular syllabi which the individual college teachers are bound to teach, even if they consider some of them as irrelevant. But these problems are universal, and with effort some of those constraints may be made more flexible. My basic approach in this lecture would be to outline some of the basic issues associated with teaching economics in the most fruitful manner should the management problems are taken care of. Let us start with students.

While the students are at the receiving end of the teaching programmes, it is this group for which the teaching effort is supposedly garnered and they are directly affected by the other partners, namely teachers' decision regarding what to teach and how to teach. Only in the case of extreme populist democratisation, do students exert their power to influence the course content – a situation which we in India seldom experience. In fact, the decision of the teaching community has far reaching consequences on the stock of knowledge of the student throughout their life. If the students are not given a proper and full picture of the subject, either through oversimplification or by partial or inaccurate representation, they will not be able to make use of it properly and in a market economy they will simply be competed out. This is related to the question of what is being taught, whether that is relevant or not. This does not, however, mean that whatever stuff is in demand in the market would be taught by teachers. But the teachers, definitely have, an obligation of training the students of Economics with those stuff that they will require to use in explaining real life situation when they are called upon to act as professional economists, not as accountant or managers. For example, with the onset of economic reforms in our country, concepts like fiscal deficits, revenue deficit primary deficit, repo rates and reverse repo rates are widely used to analyse the policy interventions by the government, and students of economics in our country are to be exposed and trained in these concepts and their use in the Indian economy at either the undergraduate or the postgraduate level. But there is definitely a case against spending of lot time and energy on Permanent Income Hypothesis (PIH), its various estimation problems and disseminating general knowledge about who has said what about PIH in the Indian context. This is for the simple reason that such hypothesis or work on them does not in any way help understanding the working of our economy, nor for that matter, of any economy. It has been cultivated its purpose of explaining the long-term constancy of savings-income ratio—a phenomenon considered puzzling to theorists trained in Keynesian consumption function. A much more meaningful exercise would perhaps been to acquaint the students of economics with the problems of national income accountings, estimation of savings investment and gross capital formation in India as well as the behaviours of money and credit markets and the integration of these monetary variables with the real variables in the context of economic policy-making in India. Students of economics of our country are not required to read the Sukhamoy Chakraborty committee report, even when they specialize in Monetary Economics, and therefore do not know the mechanism of monetary targeting often attempted by the Reserve Bank of India as a part of its stabilisation exercise. Here the teachers of economics have a definite role to play. There are many instances of teaching some stuff to students of Economics, which a student studies only to obtain marks and therefore cannot have any use of them. Thus we often find that even students carrying high percentage of marks often fail to tackle concrete economic problems—theoretical or practical – at research or professional levels, sometimes they even lose the common sense of explaining the real life of which economics is supposedly an integral part. Debates have been raised about the role of course contents in causing such a pathetic state of affairs for the students of economics. Economics teaching, it is felt, must take a new look. We shall touch on this debate later.

In my opinion, any approach to studying and teaching economic is very much dependent on the interactions and relationship between the teaching community and the scholars who attempt to extend the frontiers of knowledge in the subject. Had not Adam Smith written his *Wealth of Nations* or Keynes his *General Theory* or Hicks his *Value and Capital* or *Capital and Time* or even Paul Samuelson on varying controversial areas of economic theory. Teachers of Economics in country would not have much to offer to the students in their class lectures, either in terms of course materials or enunciation of basic principals. This has arisen in almost all the cases because we the teachers of economics in India, have seldom attempted to say something concrete and new on the subject. We may in general be cursory critique of existing theories, yet our creative works, barring a very limited few conceptions, fail to constitute a part of economics literature which other could refer and utilize. Thus if we need to teach neoclassical economics, we are bound to teach what the great thinkers in that tradition have already said. If one has a penchant for adopting a Marxian method of inquiry to the working of our economic environment and its several interpretations, we hardly have our own substantial products included in our syllabi. Therefore, whether our relevant economics is Indian Economics or Economic Theory, bourgeois economics or radical political economy, the problem remains: barring few exceptions, most of the teachers in Economics have to depend for content and methodology on what have been or are being developed elsewhere under very different condition. This bankruptcy is fundamentally due to the unhealthy dichotomy between teaching activity and research (in pure fundamental sense) activity as it exists in our country.

This hiatus, in a sense, is both historical and cultural (once again exceptions exist). We therefore in effect teach our students only old established results, which may be somewhat useful or otherwise, but which does not enable students to contribute meaningfully or fruitfully to the development of the subject. We do not in general produce good researchers, because in our endeavor to maintain *status quo*, we cultivate their ignorance. The subject therefore grows in spite of us and we and our students (unless they migrate to foreign universities) remain only in the periphery. Of course, this does not definitely mean that research activities in Indian in the field of Economics are not much. In fact, they are many and that often pose problems. Marginal variations here and there an old hackneyed themes are usually tried out in various research projects or Ph.D. work and most of the time mechanical applications of certain theoretical set of models lead to confusing and sterile type of results. The subjects does not advance an inch by such endeavor and the students, after passing out, do not and cannot strike fresh grounds. This does not of course imply that whatever additional information is published, either on theoretical or applied economic problems, should be taught, for the simple reason that most of them are bad or non-informatics. But whenever specific innovations crystallize into positive shape and expand the domain of overall economic thinking, the students should not be denied access to it on the plea that they are developed in the West. Either get involved into positive research or borrow and adopt new research into your training programme such that the students extend the state of knowledge further in future. Unless and until teaching and research activities are meaningfully integrated, the void is likely to continue and the debate about appropriateness or otherwise of the course content in Economics (and elements) will continue to be judged from the point of view of who has said what or from the viewpoint of some preconceived notion of what is relevant. Not everything that real is necessarily relevant, and the notion of relevance also evolves over time. If the state of research in the imperfect competition fails to portray the behaviour of various economic agents under alternative forms of markets, teaching of general equilibrium theory at some stage of education of economics is still the relevant study, although in reality there are various imperfections in market mechanism. Again, implication of the theory of general equilibrium would be incomplete to the students and would-be researchers unless the various pitfalls in the paradigm of perfect competition and attempts to rectify them are not pointed to them by the teachers. If the teachers of economics do not appreciate the relevance of integration between research (in real sense) and teaching, the present sorry state of affairs would alas continue.

Of course, a lot of institutional and infrastructural bottlenecks need be reformed before such a fruitful enmeshing of teaching and research can take place. The principle of second-best or the best is perhaps a compromise solution in most cases when such necessary conditions are not fulfilled. But as I have argued, these problems are not specific to Economics teaching alone. Let us therefore concentrate on some specific issues in teaching of Economics. First, the dichotomy between qualitative economics *vs.* quantitative economics or between 'history *vs.* equilibrium' as Joan Robinson put it, need be tackled. It is erroneous to argue that whatever is quantitative application-oriented and therefore meaningful, because they needs to know what to quantify and why certain results are acceptable or not, on the basis of sound grounding of certain qualitative principles. Postulates, if any are bound to be abstractions and hence somewhat unreal. And reality is much too complex and varied than can be approximated by the tools of quantitative economics only. Equilibrium economics, once again, has to be judged from the perspective of purposeful abstraction rather than a description of our everyday economic life. Students can appreciate the limitations of disequilibrium under rationing and underutilisation of capacity when these are discussed along with general equilibrium analysis. Perhaps going back to Hick's *Value and Capital* would be still more useful to the students of neoclassical economic theory. We in most cases teach economic history merely as a catalogue of economic events, not much (if at all) attention is given to the study of the theoretical structure within which meaningful explanations of economic history can be found. But I am not sure how many of our postgraduate students are exposed to the works of John Hicks, Karl Polyani, Joseph Schumpeter and Karl Marx on the methods of studying economic history. I shall not be surprised if even one percent of our students do not require to study them in their P.G. course in Economics.

Secondly, there is an obsolescence problem and the time constraint within which a course has to be conducted. The subject itself is growing at phenomenal rate in various fields and not all the ideas that were being developed are totally useless. In fact, some of them do strengthen our understanding of economic processes. If the problem of catching up is to be solved, then the course may become unmanageable and heavy, if training fails to reach the students to the frontiers, at the research level, the students are at sea – they know too little. So the choice is between too much and too little. A careful balancing would require us to take account of the generalised obsolescence of certain areas. Let us leave them and strike fresh grounds. Even if we do that, time is a genuine constraint. For example, if one tries to give the students' idea of the state of macroeconomics today, certain theoretical propositions are to be discussed with their nuances and that too is heavy enough. A detailed and sophisticated treatment may be reserved for the special paper level—but the general students must have a clear idea about the issues and propositions and their implications for the debate on national economic policy. It must also be remembered that in designing a course, sufficient scope must be given to the students for intensive study, and spoon-feeding at the P.G. level must be avoided. This may be ensured if the subjects, rather than survey articles or cooked versions are taught and they are asked to make their own-surveys-dissertation writing at the M.A. level can thus provide a scope for self-training. Group/seminar classes or problem-solving at the tutorials can also very highly rewarding—teachers of Economics are to spend much more time with their students and at libraries than is usually given now and the entire teaching activity needs to be carefully planned.

Two further sets of problems we often face with respect to our students in general. They hardly have to read the various government documents like the RBI Bulletin or Economic Surveys or the Budget of the government. They prefer summary views because we teachers also prefer such synopsis treatment in the answer scripts. Demand therefore creates its own supply. We hardly ask our students to find out what information is required to establish a given result and given a set of information as available from the government documents, how to interpret them. Too much emphasis on final results grades are responsible for this. Thus a student with first class M.A. degree in Economics often does not have even as ideas of how to tackle an economic problem. We may have techniques, computers in plenty, but minus the acquaintance with the data frame and the basic training to analyze them, products of economics departments cannot but be useless and with that teaching of economics, in the long-run, cannot but be bankrupt.

Secondly, our students are knowledgeable otherwise. But if one asks them how is India placed among the other third world countries or in the world economy or what are the specific institutional domains within which a LDC has to operate, they usually look blank. This is due to the insufficient attention given to such set of problems in our course context, and even where we do discuss these problems we expect our students to have a summary view for their examinations. We often forrget that the basic purpose of higher education in Economics is not to turn out omniscient bureaucrat, but good economists who would be able to analyze the evolving nature of world economy and be able to read its implications for the Indian economic development. Our course content should pay sufficient attention to this area.

Perhaps the most pathetic part of teaching Economics in India has been that the teaching professional is often found plagued with incoherent and ambiguous perceptions about alternative paradigms in Economics available and the sterile disputes over methodological questions. Thus we often see that the problems of economic transformation of 'crisis of accumulation in World Capitalism'. Students do not have scope to figure out the structure of present-day world economy—its trade and financial arrangement and how a LCD is placed in the overall scenario, and yet they are told about the 'conspiracy theory' of world imperialism exploiting the neo-colonies. This in my opinion, is a dangerously designed approach to economic education. Such an approach produces make-believers who chant mantras like their preachers without understanding what is what. A fruitful study of the principle of political economy cannot be undertaken (and also should not be undertaken) without prior understanding the concrete social reality—otherwise verbiage and stupidity replace scientific enquiry. Let us take another example. All of us know that competitive models are at best good abstractions to study certain economic principles as a 'designed experiment', but in reality business behaviour are by and large imperfectly competitive (of various forms). Therefore, whenever certain results about the working of Indian industries (say) do not conform to the text-book versions of the theory of perfect competition, we find a general tendency to denounce economic theory in general ('poverty of theory' is perhaps the expression used quite often). At best the students are told the sources of imperfections, in the institutions and policies of the country. But they are not usually told how such results as may seem counter-intuitive, can be rationalised in terms of a set of logical consistent theories of corporate behaviour regarding pricing, output and growth, and the financial decisions of large business firms. In fact, modern theories of imperfect competition have gone a long-way to explain the apparently surprising results, but then these theoretical structures are unusually kept outside the scope of syllabi in Economic theory and thus our students only know where the results of text-book economics go wrong, they have no idea why such things happen and what sort of theoretical refinements may be made explain them. An economist who knows only to denounce the existing theories because real life experienced do not confirm them, but not to analyze the alternative theoretical underpinnings of such real life phenomenon, is only a poor economist. He is the predict of bad investment, bad teaching, poor reading and is bound to be mentally sterile. Economics teaching in India in general is crippled because many of us (teachers) belong to such category.

There has been a tendency sometimes to simplify certain results in capsular forms, which by their nature, are complex and need be studied only in detail. The argument that is given to support such distortion of results is that good reading materials are not in general available. Paucity of genuinely good textbooks is definitely a problem. But the market textbooks on various branches in Economics perhaps oversupplied with 'trashes'. It is also true that our best minds so far concentrated on writing papers and treatises of international standards and did not pay much attention to writing good textbooks for B.A. and M.A. students. While every effort to raise the social consciousness of our great talents in economics would be welcome, there are many other short-run measures that can be contemplated to improve teaching standards. One simple way is for the government or the U.G.C. to subsidize good textbooks written by foreign authors and to arrange their Indian reprints. Infant industry argument for protection to domestically produced trashes should be abandoned strictly. Secondly, many of the teaching materials could be distributed free to colleges and universities by the documentation centers aided by Central and State governments. For this minimisation of heterogeneity in curriculum is required. But the most important way to appraise the teaching community of the latest development is the subjects and issues involved is to organize seminar/summer classes where experts in the discipline would undertaken the responsibility of education of teachers. In India, we have some internationally acclaimed scholars in Economics, and the government and the UGC, etc. must have sufficient vision to transmit knowledge to the teachers of economics in remote places. But then all this requires a fundamental changes regarding our educational system and in the attitude of those who govern. For teaching Economics, teachers and books are required, knowledge being ever-expansive, some sort of technical progress in these two vital inputs are also essential, but a lot depends on the form of the production function, here the attitude of managers, organizers and the so-called 'poors' in the subject and most importantly the bureaucrats who dictate.

Finally, I would like to say something about our method of evaluation. The standard practice has been that the students are supposed to vomit faithfully whatever is being fed in the class lectures and they are assigned some numbers in each paper. The overall performance is obtained by aggregating these marks and a student is declared first class if he obtains 60% or more. This approach to evaluation poses some problems and to my mind, it is most unscientific. When a teacher evaluates an answer-script of a particular paper he assigns numbers according to his own judgment of what is good or bad. For each such paper, therefore, there are subjective/value judgments of different teachers and by aggregating these marks we basically add non-comparable unique value judgments which is not legitimate in principle. This practice is also common in the examination of other subjects, but in Economics where we spend considerable time in talking the students about the problem of obtaining social preference from individual preferences and the impossibility of making interpersonal comparisons, such a practice runs contrary to our economics training. Where Grade system is introduced, grades are also given on the basis of some numbers and their aggregates. A more scientific approach would have been obtained if we introduce continuous evaluation system, through group classes, seminar discussions and term-paper assignments. In such a case, it is possible to have an idea about the continuous progress of the student in specific courses and his general ability to tackle economic problems without memorizing for the final examination. It is time that we take a fresh look at evaluation system and evolve pattern by which the student of Economics will be able to enjoy every bits of the subject rather than being preoccupied with the preparation for the final examination.

In conclusion, I like to stress the importance of taking a new look at the problems of teaching Economics in our country on all fronts—what to teach, how to teach and how to evaluate. The problems are not simple, yet not insurmountable. If our profession has to rise to the needs of changing environment and produce economists of high quality and originally, a fundamental change from what it is now appears essential. In this paper, I briefly point to some contours of this new approach to teaching Economics and the issues involved.

# Environmental Economics
## A Challenging Area of Research and Teaching

M. MISHRA AND N.C. SAHU

### I. INTRODUCTION

Environmental economics is an emerging area in the realm of economic science. Before 1970s as little attention was paid towards the interdependency of environment and economy, this area of knowledge was almost non-existent. The resource crunch in 1971 and the consequent emergence of relatively higher levels of environmental damages at the global level prompted the scholars in this field to apply economic tools to environmental science. Studies on environmental science are plentifully available; however they do not cover the economic content of environment. Similarly, early economists of the classical and neoclassical regime made specific comments about the significance of nature and environment, but did not include them in their exposition of theories. Today, people all over the world have realised that environment is not just the study of flora and fauna, but a synthesis of study of various branches of knowledge like Science, Economics, Philosophy, Ethics, Anthropology, etc. Therefore, a study of environmental economics calls for a detailed understanding about various environmental factors, their influence in the economy, their functions upon the environment, and their impacts upon the life of the people of the present and future.

Environmental economics is a distinct branch of economics that acknowledges the value of both the environment and economic activity and makes choices based on those values. The goal is to balance the economic activity and the environmental impacts by taking into account all the costs and benefits. The theories are designed to take into account pollution and natural resource depletion, which the current model of market systems fails to do.

## 2. ENVIRONMENTAL POLLUTION AND ECONOMICS

Market failure has been identified as the basic cause of environmental problems (Pigou, 1920; Lindhal, 1958; Arrow, 1971; Meade, 1973; Maler, 1974; Baumol and Oates, 1975; Dasgupta and Heal, 1979). The phenomenon of externality looms large in economic analysis of environmental quality problems (Dasgupta, 1996). From the very nature of economic problem and the role of market in solving it, we can find some sort of relationship between the economic activity and the environmental pollution (Common, 1988). Environmental problems stem from two related sources of market failure (Lecomber, 1975). The first is that, environment is a public good. Environmental goods and services are provided either free or not at all, because pricing of public goods is not possible as it is not possible to determine the marginal cost of production. The second source of market failure is the involvement of externalities in the production and consumption of economic goods.

Environmental pollution is largely the result of what economists call "externalities" or "public bads", which occur through production and consumption because of a structural defect of the market economy (Baumol and Oates, 1975; Fisher and Peterson, 1976; and Cropper and Oates, 1992). Since environment is a common property resource (CPR) or a public good, externality arises on it as a 'free rider' problem. Environment as a public good is consumed in equal quantity by all in a society. A clean air is a public good whereas polluted air is a public bad. A public good is subject to the principles of non-rivalry and non-exclusion in consumption. More of consumption of a public good does not mean less of it is available to others. Similarly, consumption by one does not exclude others to consume the public good. The market process is not capable of allocating resources efficiently in the presence of externalities. However, environmental economics proposes institutional innovations to be incorporated into the market to internalise externalities (Common, 1988) which are discussed in subsequent sections.

## 3. PRINCIPLES/FEATURES OF ENVIRONMENTAL ECONOMICS

The economy-environment system is characterised by the following interrelated features:

### (a) Material Balance Principle

The process of transformation of material inputs and energy into output is better explained with the help of the laws of thermodynamics. The first two laws of thermodynamics are worth-mentioning in this context. The first law of thermodynamics, which is often referred to as the law of conservation of matter and energy says that energy, like matter, can neither be created nor destroyed, but at the same time the forms of energy can be transformed. The law stresses that the total amount of energy created through production and consumption activities must be equal to the total sum of initial energy extracted from nature. Therefore, the first law of thermodynamics implies the accounting identities of material balance model. Since matter, can neither be created nor destroyed, any economy must eventually have the same amount of materials disposed of in the form of waste (output) as it initially used in the form of raw materials (inputs) in production and consumption. We extract the inputs from the reservoirs of environment and dispose of the outputs of the same mass into the reservoirs of pollution. Thus, what we produce and consume are matter-energy throughputs, a rough measure of which is the Gross National Product (Boulding, 1966). In this physical sense, 'production' and 'consumption' are very inadequate descriptions of what producers and consumers do (or convert). Moreover, the principle explains that waste generation and environmental pollution are a pervasive problem of the human economy.

**(b) The Entropy Law**

The entropy is a measure of disorder. The law states that in a closed system, the use of matter-energy cause a one-way flow from low entropy resources to high entropy resources, from order to disorder. It implies that there are definite limits to the economic process. It shows that the environmental impacts of the economy are irreversible. The entropy of the system, being a unidirectional arrow of nature, second only to time, always increases.

**(c) The Scale Effect**

The natural environment is characterized by the existence of thresholds and discontinuities, which result in large scale damages once the thresholds are exceeded.

**(d) Uncertainty of Environmental Consequences**

One fundamental feature characterising the general economy-environment system constrained by the thermodynamics laws relates to the fact that it does not have a tendency towards stable equilibrium. The change in physical factors occurring due to economic activities sets in a series of other changes which is beyond the capacity of the natural system to revert or repair. There is a great deal of uncertainty about the role natural environment plays in supporting and receiving the effects of economic activity (Victor, 1991). In other words, for many environmental problems, it is not possible to state with certainty what consequences a particular policy will have. Environmental uncertainties cannot be considered as the minor deviations of the economic system, because environmental problems pervade through an economy. Uncertainty arises because the environment is not responsive to the physical transformation of the human economy influenced by its information and control (price) system. The environmental impacts mostly come in our lives as surprises and novel experiences. The real problem relating to the environmental consequences is not of 'risk' and thus insurance is not a feasible solution. It is a situation of genuine uncertainty, as the probability of occurrence cannot be established. Coping with uncertainty is a far more difficult challenge than risk management. Changes in physical system organised according to the entropy law are irreversible.

### (e) Institutional Failures

As we know, the economy is an element of the human society. One important feature of the current patterns of societal organisation and change is that they reflect a political economic tendency, in which the market is the predominant institution of resource allocation and regulation. The focus of the market-oriented approach is on liberalisation and internationalisation. Given this tendency, it is obvious to analyse the environmental problems as the outcome of 'market failure' (or negative externality). However, there are myriads of other constraints within the institutional arrangement of a society, which cause injury to the physical environment. While in mainstream economics market failure is seen as the entry point for a government to intervene, it has been increasingly realised now that government itself is a key source of failures in realising the social optima. In this context, Johannes B. (Hans) Opschoor (2005) has proposed that for addressing environmental problems, one should go beyond the simple categories of market failure and government failure and analyse these as cases of institutional failures, which includes a wide range of transaction failure, empowerment failure and governance failure.

### (f) Public Good and Common Property

Environmental quality is a public good. Even though man, being encapsulated within a private environment, can choose to have better indoor air quality, water quality and temperature, his public environment, where most of the economic activities are conducted, is a public good. Unlike private goods, public goods are characterised by non-rivalness and non-excludability. Many environmental goods are also referred as the commons, common property resources or common pool resources (CPRs) and open access resources (OARs). The peculiarity common to all these is that of weak property right and inadequate legal protection against overuse and misuse. Professor Garrett Hardin has captured the essence of this phenomenon in the evocative phrase of the Tragedy of the Commons in 1968. The tragedy is often described as an environmental problem of distance in decision level. What is optimal from an individual perspective is not optimal from a social perspective. The individuals take a decision, which is collectively harmful.

## 4. SIGNIFICANCE OF STUDY FOR THE FUTURE

This branch of economics has great significance because of the contemporary environmental issues that gains importance day-by-day. The important global externality "Climate Change and Global Warming" draws everybody's attention and to which environmental economics has solutions and policy measures. The ideology of sustainable development is not less important and environmental sustainability is the key to it which lies with the wise and careful use of natural resources and the environment as per the guidelines delineated in environmental economics. The Millennium Development Goal, the Ecosystem Assessment, the question of Livelihood promotions and poverty eradication all fall into the premise of environmental economics. Some of the national and international efforts to promote environmental economics are explained below.

## 5. PRESENT STRENGTH IN INDIA

In India there was not much in this area of teaching and research until 1990s. It is the "India: Environmental Management Capacity Building Technical Assistance Project", 1996-2003 funded and promoted by the World Bank made the subject accessible. Establishment of the Indian Society for Ecological Economics in 1998, the establishment of the South Asian Network for Environment and Development Economics in 1999 geared up the environmental economics in the South Asia region. The following section narrates the facilities extended and infrastructure provided by different projects, institutions, agencies and organisations for the promotion of environmental economics in India.

### The India: Environmental Management Capacity Building Technical Assistance Project (EMCaB Programme)

The Ministry of Environment and Forests, Government of India implemented "India: Environmental Management Capacity

Building Technical Assistance Project" with the World Bank assistance. The specific objective of the project was to enhance environmental management capacity in selected areas of environmental management. An important area or component so identified for such capacity building or enhancement relates to Environmental Economics. The objective was to increase the capacity for the application of economic principles and tools to environmental management in India across the full range of issues such as priority-setting, cost-benefit analysis of alternative policies for pollution control, resource management, and biodiversity conservation. Achievement of this objective would be measurable in terms of the additional number of colleges and postgraduates trained in environmental economics; the number of officials, industrial managers, NGOs and others trained in environmental economics; the reach and quality of research in the field of environmental economics; and the integration of the research recommendations into environmental decision-making at the various levels of government.

The environmental economics programme consists of:

- Establishing an Environmental Economics Indicators and Project Planning Cell (EEIPPC) in the Ministry of Environment and Forests.
- Establishment of project units in environmental economics in 4 core institutions
- Support to developing an environmental economics curriculum and to preparing teaching materials, case studies, and textbooks combining India—specific case studies with examples of "best practice" from other countries.
- A faculty-upgradation program designed to train economics faculty members from across India in basic environmental economics.
- A Ph.D. Scholars workshop programme to provide an opportunity for the scholars to present their results and get feedback from experts in environmental economics and also to provide access to library, computer and faculty resources in well established centres in environmental economics.
- A program to invite environmental economics faculty

from other countries to teach and conduct research on India—specific topics.

- Training programs for practising economists and non-economists on the applications of the principles of environmental economics.
- Short-term overseas training programme for IES candidates.
- Support to selected university, institute and college libraries to expand their collections in environmental economics in the form of support for important books, journals and data bases in environmental economics.
- Support to applied research, case studies, and analysis of best practices in the area of environmental economics.
- Short-term (2-3 months) overseas research grants for researches to enable them visit well known centres in environmental economics for consultations with the experts and use the library facilities.
- Travel grants for presenting papers in international environmental economics conferences.

The implementation of this program was through four core institutions—Madras School of Economics, Indira Gandhi Institute of Development Research, Institute of Economic Growth and Indian Statistical Institute as well as through network of interested institutes. The objectives of the programme achieved through a network of four sub-committees that have divided up the work and assigned clear responsibilities under the overall guidance and supervision of the Expert Committee on Environmental Economics (ECEE).

**The Indian Society for Ecological Economics (INSEE)**

The Indian Society for Ecological Economics (INSEE), established in September 1998 and registered under the Societies Act in January 1999, is a regional society affiliated to the International Society for Ecological Economics (ISEE). INSEE's aim is to further the cause of Sustainable Development by providing a forum for continuous dialogue among scholars, practitioners, and policy analysts working on different aspects of the economy, the ecology, and the environment. It seeks to fulfil the need for a body that would facilitate interaction between scholars from various disciplines, particularly economics and ecological sciences. In the process, it strives to promote new thinking and better understanding on a range of issues of national and international interests. Through conferences, workshops, networking, and publications. INSEE works to disseminate the results of research and its policy implications to national and international bodies; governmental and non-governmental.

INSEE conducts the following activities for the promotion of teaching and research in environmental and ecological economics in India.

- Holding of INSEE Biennial Conferences.
- Organisation of seminars, workshops, policy dialogues and training programmes.
- Networking nationally and internationally through electronic and other media.
- Publication of books with selected papers presented in the Biennial Conferences.
- Publication of a newsletter for disseminating information about its activities and achievements, and about new developments in ecological economics.

For last ten years INSEE is marching ahead in discharging its duties and responsibilities with larger strength and greater enthusiasm. Already it has organized five biennial conferences and the pre-conference training programmes and workshops.

Selected conference papers are being subsequently published in edited books.

**The South Asian Network for Development and Environmental Economics (SANDEE)**

The South Asian Network for Development and Environmental Economics (SANDEE) is a regional network that uses economic tools and analyses to address South Asia's environmental challenges. It is based on the premise that solutions to economic development concerns and environmental problems are integrally linked. Thus, SANDEE brings together South Asian researchers and institutes interested in the interconnections among development, poverty and the environment. Its main goal is to build the professional skills required to enable South Asians to address local and global environmental concerns. SANDEE works in seven countries in South Asia—Bangladesh, Bhutan, India, Maldives, Nepal, Pakistan and Sri Lanka. It was launched in November 1999 and is based at IUCN-the World Conservation Union, in Kathmandu, Nepal. Its primary objectives are to:

- Strengthen the ability of researchers in South Asia to undertake research on the economics of environmental and natural resource problems;
- Support the growth of policy-relevant literature on economic development and environmental change;
- Aid the development of environment and natural resource economics in teaching and research institutions; and
- Facilitate dialogue among economists, other scholars, and policy-makers on environment and natural resource concerns.

These objectives are met through a series of research, training and information dissemination activities.

## 5. CONCLUDING VIEW

Environmental economics covers the study of the process of interdependence involved in the functioning of the economy and environmental/ecological system. It aims at sustainable promotion of human well-being. It is a methodologically open applied branch, which has been rapidly growing. The theoretical dimensions of the subject and their practical policy implications have been feeding each other in such ways that this cross-discipline is widely demanded in the classrooms, research cells and policy quarters. Several institutional efforts such as the environmental economics capacity building programmes, and the activities of INSEE and SANDEE are trying to meet the challenge of teaching and research in this trans-disciplinary field. But the core of the environmental economics paradigm is still considered as a dissent on the mainstream economics orthodoxy. There is an emergent need to synthesise the essence of this discipline with economic science at all levels. This will render economics a better friend of the earth and the humanity.

## References


Arrow, K.J. (1971), Essay in the theory of risk bearing; Chicago, Markham Publishing Company.

Baumol, W.J. and W.E. Oates (1975) The Theory of Environmental Policy: Externalities, Public Goods and the Quality of Life, Englewood Cliffs, Prentice Hall.

Common, M. (1988), Environmental and Resource Economics: An Introduction, London, Longman Group UK Ltd.

Cropper, M.L. and W.E. Oates (1992), "Environmental Economics: A Survey", *Journal of Economic Literature,* Vol. 30, pp. 675-740.

Dasgupta, P. (1996), "The economics of the environment", *Environment and Development Economics,* 1(4), pp. 387-421.

Dasgupta, P.S. and G.M. Heal (1979), "Economic Theory and Exhaustible Resources, Cambridge, Cambridge University Press.

Fisher, A.C. and F.M. Peterson (1976), "The environment in economics: a survey", *Journal of Economic Literature,* 14(l): pp. 1-33.

Lecomber, R.T. (1975) Economic Growth *versus* the Environment, London, The MacMillan Press Limited.

Lindhal, E.R. (1958), "Some controversial questions in the Theory of Taxation" in R.A. Musgrave and A.T. Peacock (eds). *Classics in the Theory of Public Finance,* MacMillan, London.

Maler, K.G. (1974). Environmental Economics: A Theoritical Inquiry, Baltimore, M.D. John Hopkins University Press for Resources for the Future.

Meade, J.E. (1973), The Theory of Externalities, Geneva, Institute Universetaire de flautes Etudes Internationales.

Pigou, A.C. (1920), Economics of Welfare, London, MacMillan.

Victor, P.A. (1991), "Uncertainty and Irreversibility Indicators of Sustainability: Some Lessons from Capital Theory, *Ecological Economics,* 4, p. 202.

# Economics Research in Indian Colleges

REKHA JAGANNATH

Research need not be connected with Academics and industry. It is an effort/response of dynamic mind towards exploring the world around him/her.

Research has been interpreted differently in different Economies and in different types of institutions at different times. In developed economies the term is used to indicate any in-depth attempt to study specific deliberately demarcated aspects of any particular concept. The concept then gets demarcated into Business research and academic research. Business and industrial research needs to end up in innovations. As Economics falls under both business and theoretical disciplines, it could focus on either of the two methods. Academic research is likely to be focused on the following short-term and initial research activities:

- Publishing research papers, organizing and participating in regional, National and International workshops, Conferences and Seminars in the area and theme of interest or specialisation.

- Guiding doctoral and M.Phil students.
- Taking up research projects that focus on hypothesis testing or tackling issues of policy implications.
- Innovations leading to patenting/policy changes.

Last two categories of research are of great significance in social Sciences. They provide solutions at micro level to firms and households and at Macro-level to policy-makers and International decision-making bodies.

India is currently spending around 1.14% of GDP for R&D as a whole on academic research. India's national aggregate gross expenditure on research and development (GERD) is about 5.5 billion Euros in 2005. Over the last decade, a dominant proportion of GERD, around 70% to 75%, is met by the government sources and the rest from private enterprises. In PPP terms, it works out to be about 24 billion Euros. India's position is above countries such as Brazil, Mexico, and South Africa but is however behind China which spent 81 billion Euro in R&D in PPP terms in 2006, after United States at almost 214 billion Euros in 2006.

Future of human resources and success of innovation in the above areas are dependent on the strength of higher education and research in the university sector. Higher educational institutions witnessed considerable growth in the post-independence period after 1947. From 20 universities in 1947 the number increased to over 361 universities and 17625 colleges affiliated to various universities in the country in 2005.

There are now 20 Central Universities, 217 State Universities, 106 Deemed to be Universities, and 13 Institutes of National Importance established through Central legislation and 5 institutions established through State legislation. The number of colleges increased from 500 in 1947 to 17,625 in 2005, indicating twenty-six-fold increase. This huge structure of higher education has made India one of the largest service provider in global higher education.

But the research output by colleges of this type is very low due to several exigencies. Some important ones among them are discussed below.

**Constraint of Permissions Galore**

Till the 10th Plan all these types of research was far fetched for College teachers and was considered as almost the crowning prerogative of Universities. Permission was to be taken from the directorate of collegiate education and the university concerned after the permission of the principal of the college to apply for any project. So practically very few faculties closely knit with the university/Directorate of Collegiate Education could involve in taking up research projects.

Even at the Universities, the same challenge surfaced with some differences. There are several managements of colleges which have the opinion that Social Science research creates idle capacity as it does not generate concrete output, particularly during early stages. They emphasize that their institutions should focus on making their students to score high in the examinations by replicating a set of answers. At College it is though to be their prime responsibility. It is felt that Universities will later inculcate research bend.

In the Universities, the faculty of Colleges can apply only with the permission of the Registrar of the University after the approval of the head of the department and the Dean of the Discipline and the Principal of the institution. So, the quantity of research output in the Universities has always been more and better than at the college level but it is still inadequate considering the faulty nature in the Universities even if not compared to that in the developed economies.

**Complacence**

Most of the faculty are bogged down by teaching and related evaluation and feed back. They are also balancing heir family life and their Faculty career. As such they cannot find time to involve in research projects which demand discipline, unlimited time, persistence and passion to work at all stages of a research project cycle. It is enough for them to teach and be at home and not do anything else about academics throughout their career. As one progresses in years of experience, more knowledge empowerment and expertise in theory ferments to conceive research projects which apply theory to practical challenges. But a major proportion of faculties tend to be more and more complacent. Ideas do not blossom from senior faculty due to monotonous, repeated lectures for years.

**Lack of Inclination for Research**

| *Faculty* | *Number of Doctorates Awarded* | | | | | |
|---|---|---|---|---|---|---|
| | *2002-03* | *2001-02* | *2000-01* | *1999-00* | *1998-99* | *1997-98* |
| Arts | 5034 | 4524 | 4398 | 4280 | 4231 | 4256 |
| Science | 4497 | 3955 | 3727 | 3885 | 3832 | 3896 |
| Commerce/Management | 857 | 728 | 621 | 571 | 567# | 517# |
| Education | 554 | 420 | 399 | 364 | 363 | 310 |
| Engineering/Technology | 243 | 219 | 221 | 228 | 225 | 195 |
| Medicine | 243 | 219 | 221 | 228 | 225 | 195 |
| Agriculture | 1042 | 838 | 889 | 787 | 732 | 806 |
| Veterinary Science | 153 | 110 | 110 | 146 | 136 | 101 |
| Law | 138 | 110 | 105 | 74 | 74 | 75 |
| Others | *436 | 336 | 296 | 238 | 225 | 255 |
| Total | 13733 | 11974 | 11534 | 11296 | 11067 | 11107 |

* Others includes music/fine arts, library science, physical education, journalism, social work, etc.
$ Provisional.
# Only commerce.
*Source*: UGC Annual Report of Different years.

Not all faculties have the mind that probes deep into the concepts they lecture on and delve into the applications and consequences connected to them. They stop at understanding the concept as much as is necessary for student needs and not anything beyond that. Many do not read more than one basic book to teach their wards. The senior teachers think they know everything in the curriculum and teach without updating till retirement as they think there is no time to deliver what they already know and it is clear that there is no room for updated information. There are many teachers who do not even deliver the lessons but spend their whole teaching tenure in dictating notes for the students to learn by-heart and replicate in the exams.

## Language Constraint

Most of the Colleges and Universities are bogged down by vernacular languages such that they are not even capable of generating a research paper. Most of the time the faculty teaching in different languages cannot meet and discuss themes as they cannot communicate or does not like to communicate with teachers of other languages at all. Moreover, applying for a research project in English and succeeding to get the project grant is very formidable task for this faculty in both colleges and universities. It is imponderable to think of such teachers carrying forward any research project till its hypothesized end.

**No Incentives**

Research projects are considered as a co-curricular activity taken up when there is no curricular effort. It is not the first priority as curricular evaluation takes the lead. They get their time bound promotions if they continue to teach and evaluate for a particular number of years. The work of researchers is often obscure. Only when the project findings are applied at the macro-level or when they get some award for it, media gets to recognize and highlight them to project them to the community. Most of the research activities are not even given hearing and are not understood by the normal faculty members. So their work often goes unrewarded in all ways.

**Fear of Failure**

Generally, college faculty think that research is the property of Universities and research Units and too high for College faculty. There is a feeling that the available academic matter and environment is insufficient to go on research projects. It is also the impression that the recognized research bodies and funders will not support college research projects. They would rather vouch for Universities. There is a opinion that the findings of college faculty will not be taken seriously by authorities due to limited exposure compared to the Universities and research institutes. So, it is thought to be safe to evince interest in curriculum related teaching and evaluation activities to be appreciated by the fraternity.

**Outdated Research Methodology**

Most of the research in Indian Colleges and even Universities follows application procedure and even methodology which is not accepted in the developed nations. Such methology does not also lead to much value addition both in terms of theory building a and in terms of dealing with policy issues or community economic problems, in the connected environment. College faculty members who attempt to take up research projects are not familiar with software packages available for data collection, data analysis and report designing and report writing.

#### Dearth of Infrastructure

Access to infrastructure is essential to carry on research activities successfully. The space provided for library itself is insufficient. Development of the library is not prioritized over the examination-related activities. Many of the Colleges/Universities of India do not have their own and up dated physical and human infrastructure for research in humanities. They do not have updated National and International publications in the library. In lieu of this, there needs to be internet library membership like that of 'Justor'. This is far fetched.

#### Dearth of Funds

Research activities need clearly allotted funds. Researchers with clear vision for projects need to be out into research wing. More over research in Economics lie in other humanities results are not visible in the early years. So fear of creating idle capacity keeps away managements of Colleges and much less extent the Universities from ploughing-in funds into research projects and related activities. UGC funds extended for research is inadequate to meet all the infrastructural and salary needs of research.

#### Politics in Universities

Universities have become hubs of training in politics. So the faculty members and office-bearers of the Universities do not evince much interest in ling run interest like research. So the college faculty having much wider spread of knowledge base should be given chances to take research opportunities that arise due to policy needs and knowledge gaps.

#### Low Volume of Funds Flow

There is an increase in the number of colleges and Universities in India. The higher education structure has become more complex with a wide variety of non-university bodies increasing in number. Although assistance is provided through UGC to about 160 State Universities and 5625 colleges through development grants, due to the budgetary constraints the funding is low and insufficient affecting the quality of interventions.

To overcome above mentioned situation, there is need for fund raising by researchers themselves. This is done only by the faculty members who are fired with passion for research and not all. There are sufficient sources of funds for research in the economy and in rest of the world available for Indians. Knowledge of sources of funds for research and the procedures related to this are almost beyond the reach of all College and University faculty. Only those who search for the sources of funds do surely succeed as funds do exist earmarked for the purpose in the corporate circles, International agencies and the Government itself.

### Examination and Documentation-based Education System

Most of the higher education system in India, as much as the school education revolves around examinations and marks cards. So, Colleges and Universities have become teaching shops churning out graduates and postgraduates. Very few of these students take to research. Driven by this, teachers at large find no reason to evince interest in research related activities.

There is need for inclusive research: Colleges in the rural areas need to change, modernize and standardize to familiarize with the accepted methods of research India in the last decade has taken advantage of globalisation Innovation and developed a huge ICT software knowledge sector with unique innovation strategies. This has enabled India to capture a good deal of knowledge based services market in the world but the major challenge in the coming decade is to bridge 'digital divide' within the country.

Semester scheme adopted all over higher education, flowing American system of higher education has led to increase in documentation which has eaten into the time that faculty could allot for content enhancement through learning, development and research.

Added to these maladies, Social Science faculty is very often discriminated against natural Science faculty while extending funds and while prioritizing recognition for all purposes.

Research institutions approved centre for research do not readily support, collaborate and network with college teachers.

There is an air of pseudo superiority when they deal with college faculty.

Research has not been among the main aims of higher education after independence: 'Indian higher education system caters to wide varieties of needs and choices make up for the diversity of its society'.

## Present Scenario

Indian research system and structure of governance can be characterized as a 'top-down model' but it is an open model with democratically centralised system. About 8800 affiliated colleges of State universities, mainly undergraduate colleges, are technically under the purview of UGC but do not get assistance as they do not meet the minimum eligibility norms in terms of physical facilities and human resources. During the Eleventh Plan, about 6000 colleges and 150 universities with focus on under served areas will be strengthened to enable these institutions to fulfil the criteria for UGC assistance. Each college and university will be provided Rs. 2,000,000 and Rs. 10,000,000, respectively, based on Detailed Project Report.

**Institutional Capacity Expansion**

| *Capacity Expansion* | *1950* | *2008* |
|---|---|---|
| Number of Universities | 25 | 431 |
| Number of Colleges | 700 | 20,677 |
| Number of Teachers | 15,000 | 5.05 lakh |

As the consequence of the factors discussed above, very few teachers from College and Universities initiate research projects. There is preference to conduct seminars, workshops and Conferences, in addition to taking research projects as they involve less complex processes. The number of faculty members who apply for research projects is itself low. Therefore, there is low turn out of value also when the projects are taken. The number of research projects taken up by faculty members of humanities, is far less than that in pure Sciences. But the research projects taken have been increasing over the decades. There is better possibility of taking up research projects at University level. But the number of projects taken by University faculty members is not much more than that of Colleges.

| | |
|---|---|
| Research | 1% |
| Diploma Certificate | 1% |
| Postgraduate | 9% |
| Undergraduate | 89% |

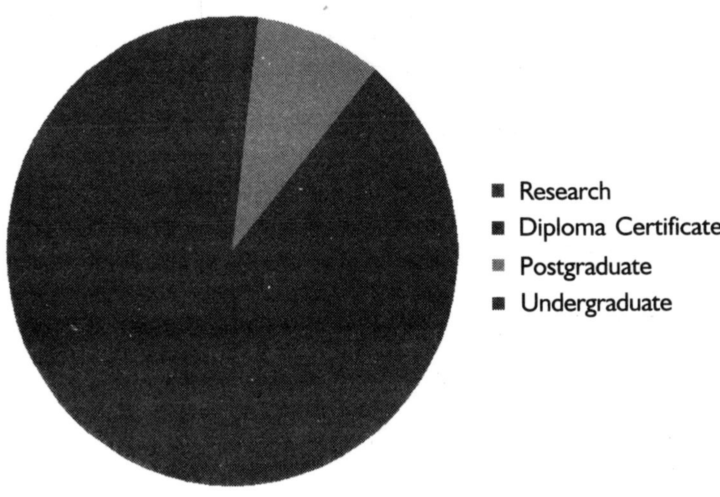


*Source*: UGC Annual Reports, 2006-07.

| | |
|---|---|
| Arts | 46% |
| Agriculture | 1% |
| Medicine | 3% |
| Engineering/Technology | 7% |
| Education | 1% |
| Commerce/Management | 18% |
| Veterinary Science | 1% |
| Law | 3% |
| Others | 1% |

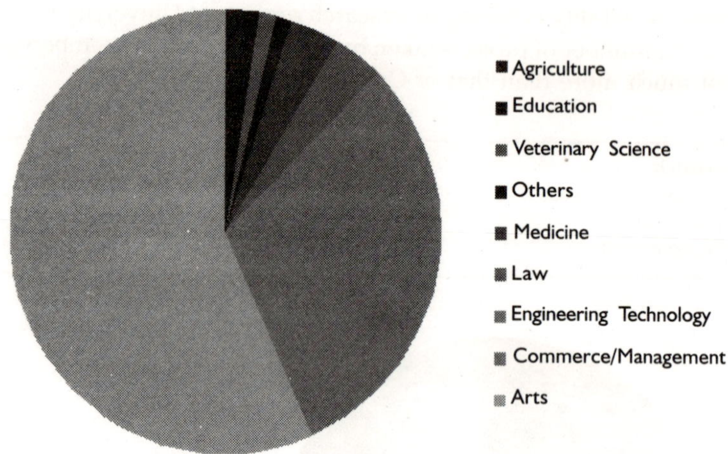


*Source*: UGC, Annual Reports, 2006-07.

**Summary of the Results Observed in the Teacher Survey**

| *Sl. No.* | *Findings* | *% of total* |
|---|---|---|
| 1. | Not doing any kind of research together with teaching | 52 |
| 2. | Expressed difficulty to mange teaching and research | 68 |
| 3. | Having complaints about career advancements | 44 |
| 4. | Unable to get funding for research | 16 |
| 5. | Lack of administrative support | 52 |
| 6. | Having international collaboration | 01 |
| 7. | Research projects undertaken | 28 |

*Source*: UNESCO Headquarters, Paris, 29 November-1st December, 2006.

At the dawn of Independence Universities and Colleges were the hub of research along with teaching. But in 1960s a small number of institutions were started to take up research alone in a specialised manner. This has made Universities and Colleges mere teaching shops. The specialised research institutes are thought to be responsible for all research in the country and Universities think it is their responsibility to generate students ready for these research centers and not replicate them.

**Need to Retain Research Component at College Level**

All well qualified intellectuals cannot be absorbed by the university. So there are knowledgeable faculties at college level who need to express their spirit of inquiry. So they have to be provided channels for this investigative knowledge empowerment.

At present, Colleges are well exposed to several avenues like Corporate bodies, MNCs, FIIs and international Donors. So they can take up research projects efficiently. Several value adding ideas will go unexplored if they are not given scope at college level. Corporate Social responsibility funds are extended for Social Science research which improves community well-being.

Towards millennium development goals there is need for higher volume of research involvement by academics of higher education as they are sensitized about the meaning and depth of societal challenges.

Levels of restriction to work efficiency in the form of files to be moved and documents for application are less at college-level than at the University. So, there is greater scope for submission of proposals to bodies that conduct perennial research in Social Science issues.

Colleges have become equally competent as Universities with internet provision and more revenues over the years, compared to that of Universities. The provision of Postgraduate courses to be run at college level has also enabled more specialised knowledge dissemination at college level. This empowerment will be scuttled if research is not allowed to blossom at college level.

Persistent Research at college level by faculty will churn out expertise which could be feeders to research at the Universities.

**Context**

Current developments in the economy, community as well as changes in the attitudes of the people have led to compulsion to allow research in Colleges.

Globalisation has led to greater contact between India and rest of the world. Restrictions to inflow and outflow of faculty have been reduced to allow for knowledge transfer and knowledge dissemination throughout the globe. So the number of faculty members who go on delegations and guest lectures to rest of the world has increased. So also there is an increased inflow of foreign intellectuals who perpetuate knowledge into the economy.

**Sustainable Development**

There is impending urgency of providing climate security with global warming. Development through the promotion of livelihood practices ensuring Indian higher education is sensitive to the issue of sustainable sustainability, reducing poverty, educating women and children and in fostering respect and interest in environmental protection. Universities across India are getting more sensitive to the generation, application and transfer of knowledge about the environment and ways of sustaining it for the future. In this direction there is need to give scope to the investigating skills of college faculty members.

**Inclusive Growth**

The sections of the economies suffering from inequities are growing larger. There is gender bias, regional inequities, color discrimination, caste discrimination and rural-urban bias along with language bias. So there is need for inclusive approach which can promote research into the complex inequities towards inclusive research for growth and development. The population size of faculty being larger at college-level with possibility of knowledge empowerment, they need to be given platform to contribute to R&D.

**Measures to Develop Research and Development in Colleges**

UGC is trying its best to inculcate research spirit in the teaching fraternity of higher education. XIth plan document UGC grants are extended to teachers of Colleges and Universities for minor and major research projects. Commission approved 96 major research projects in Humanities and Social Sciences.

College faculty members are required to do two refresher courses at research institutes as required for promotions, so that they are exposed to research environment. They can develop relevant network with research institutions during refresher courses, so as to culminate in research collaborations. Principals of Colleges are required to hold a doctorate so that they know the significance of research in academics. There are several changes in the structure and functioning of higher education after globalisation. Till 31st March 1997 nearly 1.14 lakh college teachers participated in refresher courses. 42,000 teachers participated in orientation courses.

During the Eleventh Plan, these colleges and universities will be provided one-time assistance at the rate of Rs. 1,000,000 and Rs. 5,000,000, again based on DPR. This support will be subject to the matching commitments on funding and reforms from the Centre, States, and institutions.

India already has many highly educated and vocationally qualified people who are making their mark, domestically and globally in research and development (R&D). The proportion of those who hold doctorates in arts is higher in arts, Sciences and commerce. But they represent only a small fraction of the total population. To create a sustained cadre of 'knowledge workers', India plans to make its education system more demand driven to meet the emerging needs of the economy and to keep its highly qualified people in the country. This means raising the quality of all higher education institutions, not just a few world-class ones, such as the Indian Institutes of Technology. Some ways of making the system more demand driven are to allow the private sector to fill the burgeoning demand for higher education by relaxing norms and through better accreditation systems for private providers of education and training. Increased university-industry partnerships to translate research into applications can yield economic value. Lifelong learning programs can be used to meet the learning needs of all, both within and outside the school system, including using distance learning technologies to expand access to and the quality of formal education and lifelong training program. India is becoming a major global source of R&D; about 100 multinational corporations have already set-up R&D centers in the country, leading to the deepening of technological and innovative capabilities among Indian firms. To facilitate this, India needs to tap into the rapidly growing stock of global knowledge through channels such as foreign direct investment, technology licensing, and so on. An important part of India's innovation system is the diffusion of modern and more efficient technologies in all sectors of the economy. India has caught the attention of the world in its innovations in areas ranging from pharmaceuticals to software. There is a need to boost traditional knowledge linking it with modern science and exploiting public-private partnerships to enhance innovations for achieving better quality of life. The social attitudes have to change so as to enable the people in the community to take the facilitates given by the reformers. Providing research facilities to college teachers enables a larger brigade in higher education to meet the above said challenges.

## Doctoral Research

The place of doctoral study in the research management assumes importance in the context of knowledge society. The institutional role of universities is recognized to explore ideas and knowledge. Doctoral level research is the chief instrument through which universities allow to cultivate knowledge and disseminate it through two domains—teaching and research. The research emerging from universities should be viewed as primarily contributing to national development. Yet at the level of practice, the share of the higher education sector in the total Research and Development (R&D) expenditure is a meager 2.97%, as per the survey conducted by Government of India in the year 1998-99. In the field of research the concentration of resources in bodies outside the universities in research, laboratories under Council of Scientific and Industrial Research (CSIR), other research institutions and industries both in the public and private sectors is responsible for a rather low expenditure on R&D in higher education sector. Low R&D expenditure in the higher education sector not only affects the doctoral level of research but also is responsible for the low level of basic research in the universities. At the same time, poor university/industry linkages have not induced doctoral education in the universities to contribute in terms of applied research either. But, the place of doctoral research cannot simply be evaluated in terms of R&D expenditure in higher education sector and its contribution in basic and applied research at the level of doctorate research alone. In India, the view is taken that successful doctoral candidates are the finest human resources; they have acquired the highest levels of knowledge in the relevant field. Success at doctoral level means the development of a continuing aptitude for independent scientific inquiry and, therefore, those with a doctorate should have great potential to serve as good teachers or scientists or leaders in all sectors of development.

The XIth Plan has various schemes to support the faculty development and research base in the universities. All these interventions will ultimately help Indian higher education system to exploit opportunities emerging from globalisation.

XIth Plan has provided provisions to extend faculty development fellowship under which individual college teachers can go on deputation to take up research projects to empower themselves with higher qualifications like M.Phil, Ph.D. and post-doctoral pursuits. Under SAP (Study Abroad Program) they can even pursue research abroad without breaking their career.

INFLIBNET is provided by UGC to information online to pursue research. This is to overcome the constraint of lack of information flow as the block to development of research spirit.

Internal fund raising is encouraged by giving half of the mobilised funds as incentive to the University. This is a significant step to encourage College teachers to garner funds from private, market, community and foreign sources of research funding.

Even retired teachers, teachers who have worked for several years under UGC and had a break are all allowed to take up projects subject to the approval of the head of the institution and final sanction of UGC.

Active teaching and thirst to update in their area of teaching promotes research. The institutions which are confident of being self sufficient in terms of administration and funds are allowed to go autonomous so as to provide flexibility in curriculum formation and lesson delivery. This gives faculty to mobilize student potential to support their research work while they themselves imbibe research attitude observing their peer groups and mentors. Of course, the provision is under the monitoring of UGC.

Even now, UGC funding is found to be a restrictive route to research funding. Social Science teachers who find UGC can now resort to funding by ICSSR, corporate funds and international support as well. The criteria for funding research by these agencies do not go by the rigid promotion structure required and signatures by authorities who are averse to research by college teachers.

**Summary of Fundings**

Over the decades after globalisation, provisions for college teachers to conduct research have better hopes. Particularly the XI plan has tried to make torrential changes in the College education structure so as to enable research amidst the other changes. Previous restrictions are largely relaxed. Funding for knowledge enhancement and research has been increased and the diversification of funding is enhanced. Still there are several impediments to College teachers in taking up research projects.

**Suggestions**

Some innovative/effective measures to be taken are such as the following:

Project-based education at college level itself will train and empower both students and teachers in current research methodology.

Discrimination between college teachers and University teachers for research funding should be totally removed. Criteria-based evaluation of proposals for funding research should be adopted.

A particular proportion of research funding allotted to Universities and Research bodies should be earmarked for the College teachers.

Research institutions and Universities which collaborate with college teachers in their projects should be given incentives.

Private and community funding should be classed on par with public funding for promotion possibility and for incentives.

Only Academics and pragmatic policy-makers should be made office-bearers Universities and Research bodies so that they promote growth of research and development.

Procedures for research funding should be made more transparent. UGC has certainly moved some paces towards this by announcing the status of the application and taking the application of those who missed out last times in the next year. But there is need for step by step transparency of movement of the application and evaluation criteria.

There is need for progressive attitude towards the applicants among the office-bearers of the Universities. Those who show animosity against the College researchers should be reprimanded and speedy disposal of research grant application files without airs needs to be given some incentive till the attitude catches up.

Taking up research projects should be made not only made compulsory for promotions in all social Science faculty but also should be made an eligibility criterion to be employed as a College teacher.

Each college should be encouraged to develop a research centre with its own vision. UGC already extends funds for infrastructure development funds. These funds must be given on priority to College Research Centers. University and Research Centers should help the development of such centers by nurturing and supporting them, instead of snubbing them. Such behaviour should be encouraged by the HRD Ministry.

Discrimination between pure Science research and Social Science research should be tackled with some measures as follows:

Interdisciplinary research should be given incentives to wade away. The Research in Social Sciences should be made feasible through implementation. Social Science Researchers should be given priority when scouting for advisors and consultants to the Ministries at the states and the GOI (Government of India).

## References

Era Watch Inventory report for India; European Commission http://cordis.europa.eu/erawatch/Sub-regional Conference of South, South-west and Central Asia on Higher Education, 25th-26th February 2009, Vijayan Bhawan, New Delhi.

UNESCO Forum on Higher Education, Research and Knowledge—Second International Colloquium on Research and Higher Education Policy held between 29 November-1st December 2006.

UGC Annual Reports of various years.

# Professional Excellence for Research Guide in Economics

R. MEENAKSHI

## Introduction

Universities are knowledge-based organisations whose functions are largely confined to teaching and research. They are designed to operate to discover and disseminate knowledge by possessing significant and relevant expertise in all disciplines. At the same time parents, governing boards, state legislatures, regional accrediting agencies and the general public are demanding greater accountability from institutions of higher education particularly in case of applied research. This is equally applicable to Economics discipline too. However, modern educational institutions of higher learning have been extremely successful in nurturing and promoting original thinkers and they are termed as professionals.

## What is Professionalism?

It is widely believed that a profession has three features: training that has intellectual and involved knowledge, as distinguished from skill; work that is pursued primarily for others and not for oneself; and success that is measured by more than the amount of financial return. Building an education community committed to professionalism ultimately may preserve those aspects of the relationship between the guide and research scholar. Professionalism is an integral quality which depends on the level and methods of mastering the different types of pedagogical activity, which in turn makes it possible for the research guide to perform the functions and secures professional mobility. The term guides' professionalism refers to pedagogical qualities and competence. These integral qualities of professionalism depend on the individual features of the research guide.

### What is Professional Excellence?

Professional excellence is not simply a matter of obtaining recognition for the work. It is not even climbing the corporate ladder in an educational institution. Developing professional excellence is a lengthy and challenging process. There are bound to be errors and misunderstandings along the way, and the goal must be to learn from them, leave them behind, and move forward with a single and concerted aim to build a strong knowledge based society of research scholars. This is possible only by a committed clan of research guides.

### The Professional Values

It is critical that the guides involve themselves in the process. While an institution may already have a clear mission statement and set of educational values, a continual re-examination of those values is important to maintain a competitive environment, and ensure that the current faculty understand and integrate those values into their daily work. Values may include newer elements such as innovation, teamwork, continuous improvement and commitment to consistent professional and organisational dedication to the shared missions and values of the institution.

### The Pattern of Higher Education in India

Indian students interested in pursuing higher studies may either directly register for Ph.D. or do a pre-doctoral program called Master of Philosophy (M.Phil.) which is either completely research based or may also include some course work. It takes lesser time to complete Ph.D. for those who have already done M.Phil. due to their exposure in formulating hypotheses and solving them in their M.Phil. work. Hence the responsibility of a research guide starts even at this level to shape the scholar to meet the requirements of the doctoral work.

**Institutions of Higher Education in India**

- The higher education system has been growing at a very rapid pace.
- Today, we have as many as 357 universities in India, out of which 20 are Central universities that are of a high caliber.
- There are many institutions of national importance such as the National Council of Applied Economic Research, Madras School of Economics, Madras Institute of Development Studies, Institute of Economic Growth and Delhi School of Economics, to name a few, which are now rated as world-class institutions.
- There are 217 State universities, at least about 30 per cent of which are of high standard.
- Of the 102 deemed universities, in both private and public sectors, at least 50 of them can be described as very good.
- In substance India has about 150 Institutions of Higher Education capable of providing Quality Research facilities.

**Activities in a Department of Economics**

Research and teaching at most of the departments of economics span the domains of managerial economics, agricultural economics, industrial organisation, international business, innovation economics and management, political economy, and entrepreneurship. Such departments contribute to theoretical and empirical research on various topics. Research is strongly focused on the development of an analytical basis that allows a better understanding and prediction of firm strategies. Major research topics include: the effects of market integration on corporate strategies, competition *versus* cooperation in strategic R&D investments, management of innovation in global firms, university-industry transfers and their impact on innovative productivity, political business strategies and business-government relations and multinational business location decisions. In case of environmental economics the activity will be around impact of environmental degradation on the human inhabitants in a select locality or environmental accounting to assess recovery of wealth from wastes. Under the field Agricultural economics the work would center on economics of select crop growth or land utilisation pattern in a select area.

**Need for Quality in Guiding Research**

A strong and effective higher education system is integral to individual success, social cohesion, progress, and national prosperity for generating a knowledge-based society. The capacity needed to help research scholars develop the ability to think critically, create, solve complex problems and master complex subject matter, is much more demanding on the guides than that needed by teachers to impart and develop routine skills. Thus research guides have to be both knowledgeable in their content areas and extremely skilful in a wide range of analytical approaches to cater for the diverse research needs of every scholar.

This process should include a number of areas as below.

- Providing high-quality research guidance calling for constantly refining the skills by interaction with professional colleagues and by specific training.
- Communicating clearly to the selected audiences, without simply presenting the data.
- Commitment to fulfil promised schedules of submitting periodical progress reports to the universities.
- Recognizing the professional limits without overstating the abilities and expertise.
- Participating in activities that help the scholars like presenting papers, publishing books, etc.

**Guides' Responsibilities**

Guides induce consistent research scholar performance as

below:

- They must remain academically authoritative and "current" in their fields.
- They must hold high expectations of all scholars, and set high standards for them
- The percentage of scholars' time spent "on-task" must be consistently high
- Preparation must be thorough and integral to their research activities.

Research guides behaving in ways consistent with these principles can expect their wards to perform more consistently, to be powerfully reinforced, thus fostering in themselves and in their peers higher morale and a sense of career excitement and commitment.

**Effective Communication as a means of Effective Guidance through Feedback**

Communication is a network of interactions. The sender and the receiver namely the guide and the scholar must have effective information interchange. A concerted listening process by the research scholar is essential for effective research work. The guide has to provide information in a manner understandable. The feedback from the scholars is possible only if they listen fully paving way for clarifying their doubts. Discussions between the scholar and the guide improve the level of understanding by the scholar helping the guide to alter his style of guidance to suit the needs of the research worker. To achieve improved guidance, the methodologies are: Feedback or evidence relating to the effectiveness of guidance, based on that evidence, conclusions for development of guidance and enhancement and a Personal Action Plan for bringing about that development and enhancement.

**Characteristics of Good Guidance**

- Good guidance is about motivating students to pursue their research activity and guiding them how to go about progressing in their activities and treating them as consumers of knowledge.

- Good guidance is about bridging the gap between theory and practice.
- Good guidance is about listening, questioning, being responsive, and remembering that each research scholar is different and entertaining without lacking in substance.
- Good guidance should care, nurture and develop their minds and talents devoting time to each.

## The Research Guide as an Organizer

Research guidance is defined as the organisation of investigative work to achieve authentic results assuming that effective outcome will take place. This situation is made up of many parts.

1. There must be a willing research worker.
2. There must be facilities like a place and time for meeting, and books and other printed materials.
3. There must be an orderly and understood procedure for presenting, discussing and evaluating.
4. There must be grading so that the guide and research scholar will know how the research activity is coming along.
5. There must be an organizer who brings these parts into a whole — in other words, the guide.
6. Hence guidance is essentially an organizer enabling research scholars to conduct research effectively for their future.

## Enhancing the Guiding and Work Effectiveness

Research guides have to improve their guiding effectiveness and communicate their expectations to their research scholars by using a comprehensive framework of work activity with specified assignments, intermittent seminars and projects. Work activities must be planned ahead of time by listing the points. Presentation skills are extremely important because they create the enthusiasm and interest that makes research scholars to be attentive. The material should be rehearsed and reviewed regularly. This will be of great help to research scholars to present their work during viva-voce.

*Involving the scholar*

The guide must get the scholar involved in identifying his research needs and outcomes. He can engage the scholar by selecting materials that require his/her direct involvement. Giving the scholars chance to their ideas and to be creative will promote effective research activity.

*Begin with what the scholar knows*

Conducting the research work is faster when it builds on what the scholars already know. By comparing the old, known information with the new ones allows them to grasp new information quicker.

*Move from simple to complex*

Research scholars find working easy if they have opportunity to master simple concepts first and then apply them to more complex ones. However, what one scholar finds simple, another may find complex. A careful assessment takes this into account and helps the guide plan accordingly.

*Accommodate the scholars' preferred learning style*

How quickly scholars finish their work depends on their intelligence, prior education, on their styles of problem-solving and their analytical ability. The guides can improve their guidance based on the scholars' preferred style and plan activities using appropriate tools.

*Allow immediate application of knowledge*

Giving the research scholars an opportunity to apply their knowledge and skills reinforces working ability and builds confidence paving way for problem-solving, feedback, and emotional support.

*Tell the research scholars how they are progressing*

Research activity is made easier when the scholars are informed of their progress. Positive feedback can motivate them to greater efforts because it makes their goal seem attainable. They must be allowed to take part in assessing their own progress and their input can guide the guide himself.

*Reward desired learning with praise*

Praising the scholars' successes gives desired goal with a sense of growing and accepted competence. Reassuring them that they have progressed well helps them retain and refine it. It ushers them to perform "Better and Still Better"

**Developing Effective Guiding Skills**

Developing effective guiding skills is important in the doctoral work since demonstrating the ability to guide others effectively is important. Doctoral students are assigned to assist a senior research scholar or in other research activities of the institution thus providing an opportunity to work closely with an experienced staff to gain exposure to the subject, learn methods for testing, grading, and providing feedback, and become familiar with different styles of investigative activities. Thus at the end of the doctoral work they get considerable experience in their area of specialisation. Due to this they attain an ability to take up teaching as a profession and thereafter become guides for other research scholars. Many resources are available in the institutions to improve their work effectiveness like regular workshops, group projects, grading, etc. Many equipments like Flip Charts, AV aids, OHPs, Power Point Presentations and methodologies like Lecture with Discussion, Brainstorming sessions and group discussions with case studies, and Worksheets/Surveys come in handy when they have to present their work before an evaluation committee for award of Ph.D.

**Professional Elements required for Guides**

To achieve professional ethics and excellence, ethical values need to be fully instilled into professional culture and practice with a defined characteristic of professionalism. This implies that the career dimensions of guides must have specific aspects of guidance which are interdependent and overlapping.

*Professional knowledge*

Guides should know and understand the fundamental ideas, principles and structure of the disciplines they guide and know how to effectively steer the student towards the goal.

*Professional practice*

Guides have to communicate effectively with their wards and establish clear goals for research. They must understand the need to evaluate their guidance and the importance of providing both formal and informal feedback to students as a stimulus to their work.

*Professional competence*

They must work closely with the institution since higher education and research activities of students indicate a shared enterprise. They uphold high professional ethics with regard to their own conduct and that of others, and respect their students and value their diversity.

*Professional relationships*

Research guides engage with different types of scholars. It is within this context that they have to design and manage problem-solving experiences and analytical abilities. They have to work productively with colleagues and other professionals to enhance the outcome of the scholars.

**Characteristics of Research Guides with Professional Excellence**

The qualities and characteristics of effective guide who demonstrate excellence in guiding are described in four categories:

*Intrinsic motivation and the ability to motivate others*

Faculty is highly motivated to achieve excellence and motivate the scholars to reach their educational goals. Faculty creates a sense of accomplishment in them when they demonstrate their ability. They instil in them the desire and self-confidence needed to improve their work.

*Interpersonal skills*

An excellent guide in a research institution interacts actively and positively with students and colleagues by providing corrective feedback. They recognize that students have different working styles and they encourage students to develop their individual learning abilities. Thus an excellent faculty is always made available to research scholars.

*Knowledge-base*

Faculties possess a broad range of intellectual skills and knowledge necessary for superior performance. They have a thorough understanding not only of their own work areas and disciplines, but also of how scholars learn and develop. These faculties share their knowledge with one another to achieve an excellent guidance process at the college and do their work in a well-prepared and well-organized manner.

**Skill at Applying that Knowledge**

They apply major principles of research work into practice as they carry out their responsibilities related to the teaching/ learning process to make them learn effectively and efficiently. They stimulate intellectual curiosity and create an interactive learning environment in which students are active learners and make them think independently.

**Journey to Excellence in Guiding**

Achieving professional excellence in research guidance is like a long journey laden with several important activities as below:

- A vision, shared values, and common goals.
- A clear understanding of the philosophy, history, and goals of research activity.
- Utilisation of the growing body of research on effective education.
- Educational leaders and governing boards create institutional cultures that encourage innovation without fear of failure.
- A renewing cycle of improvement in research institutions.

**Signs of Professional Excellence in Guides**

The private independent guide does far more than the guides in an institution. The interactions with more impact often occur outside the institution in coaching, in advising or even during an informal chatting. This is possible with external guides chosen from an institution other than where the scholar works. In these cases choosing the external guide is necessitated where a guide is not available in the place of work for the scholars who are employed in an institution or industry. Professionally excellent guides interact with research scholars in a way that keeps them consistently high-achieving and satisfied with their institutional experience. They possess:

- Knowledge of current activities in the chosen field of research process and setting high standards/ expectations for students.
- Explicit preparation for all graded events.
- Mission-consistent discipline in all instances.
- Meaningful emotional/psychological engagement with all students.
- Active support for colleagues.
- Positive contribution to professional approach with all constituent groups.
- Responsiveness to student needs.

### Recommendations to Achieve Value-based Excellence in Research Guidance

Some excellent examples of promising policies and practices in the research institutions are emerging. They cover the continuum of a research career, including:

- Recruiting talented and diverse people into the faculty profession;
- Improving guide preparation and raising licensing and certification standards for research guides;
- Providing professional support to new guides during their initial stages; and
- Improving professional development practices and accountability.

## References

Alan P. Rossiter, "In Search of Professional Excellence", Reprinted from *AICHE Journal*, February 1995.

"Achieving Excellence in the Teaching Profession", Promising Practices: New Ways to Improve Teacher Quality, September 1998.

Cornelius von Baeyer, "What's workplace ethics?", Presentation to shareholders of a European-based international industrial enterprise, Spring, 1999.

Dr. Jose and Prof. B.S. Mohanty, "Professional Ethics", Charúlatha Publications, Chennai (2004).

William B. Walstad and Sam Allgood, "Views of Teaching and Research in Economics and Other Disciplines", AEA Papers and Proceedings (2005).

Arkadev Chatterjea and Satya P. Moulik, "Doctoral Education and Academic Research (in India)", Working Papers, Cornell University ILR School (2006).

Steven C. Myers, Michael A. Nelson and Richard W. Stratton, "Assessing A Proficiency-based Economics Program: Weathering The Pérfect Storm While Thriving In A New Environment", JEL Codes: General Economics and Teaching (2008).

Steve Thornton, "Standards for Excellence, Sustainable Assessment and the Development of Teacher Identity", University of Canberra, Australia.

Standards of Instructional Excellence Report from Connecticut Community Colleges, USA.

# Training in Research in Economics for the M.Phil. and Ph.D. Degrees

V. Krishna Murthy

## INTRODUCTION

India is a developing economy. The economic stagnation and the vicious circle of poverty characterized the pre-independence Indian economy. After independence slowly but steadily there is rapid economic activity and higher levels of income under the impact of continuous economic planning.

Our present economic ailments are those associated with or arising directly from the problems of economic growth. It is highly important that the Indian scholars of M.Phil. and Ph.D. degrees understand and appreciate these problems and undertake studies to identify the variables involved in the process of economic growth and offer suggestions to remove the bottlenecks and achieve sustainable economic development.

The scholars of Indian economics have been feeling the need for proper teaching and research orientation which highlight the problems of growth and present a new approach to the study of the Indian economy. We have to discard the traditional approach to the subject and present a new study of development oriented approach of the Indian economy. This demands a strong foundation into the subject-matter of Indian economy as well as a scientific research orientation, both at macro-level and micro-level.

## EXHAUSTIVE COURSE WORK FOR RESEARCH IN ECONOMICS: M.Phil. AND Ph.D.

In course of his critique of the Report of the Fourth Review Committee (ICSSR, March 2007), Balakrishnan (2008) suggested "exhaustive course work lasting up to two years as part of the Ph.D. programme. Balakrishnan's suggestions are very good and the ICSSR Review Committee too made a similar suggestion. One strong point of IGIDR's Ph.D. Programme is its "exhaustive course work" both for regular and external candidates (part-time scholars).

The exhaustive work may include:

1. Background Knowledge of Indian Economy which consists of:
   - (i) Structure of the Indian Economy,
   - (ii) Planning and Economic Development,
   - (iii) Agriculture in the National Economy,
   - (iv) Indian Industries,
   - (v) Indian Labour,
   - (vi) The Tertiary Sector in Indian Economy.
2. Research Methodology.
3. Selected Topics in Economy Theory and Economic Policies.

## I. BACKGROUND KNOWLEDGE OF INDIAN ECONOMY

### (i) Structure of the Indian Economy

A strong foundation into the subject matter of Indian economy starts with an analysis of the Indian economy. The existence of the trap of under-development equilibrium, the basic characteristics of the Indian economy, national income and its components, the distribution of national income and consumption pattern, the study of human and natural resources in the context of economic development in India, the problems of capital formation, etc. provide a broad cross-section of the Indian economy. To have the picture of Indian economy more complete and comprehensive, the scholar should also have proper information of the sociological factors in economic development and economic transition of India with a comprehensive survey of economic policies during the last 200 years and their impact.

**(ii) Planning and Economic Development**

It is essential that the scholar understands and appreciates the rationale and philosophical basis of Indian planning, the growth of industrial policy and the growing role of the public sector in Indian economy which provide the ideological background to Indian planning. He should also have a proper review of fifty years of planning, the consideration in the formulation of various plans and the pattern of financing the plans. Besides, the role of external assistance in Indian economic development, the significance of price policy in a developing economy like India and the need for mobilizing and augmenting the marketable surplus which are the key factors to be operated upon by the planning authority in view of the needs of economic development are to be discussed by the scholars among themselves during discussion and seminar sessions.

The purpose of having a thorough knowledge of planning and economic development is to develop the skill of presenting a comprehensive view of the perspectives and problems of Indian planning, the lessons to be drawn from our experience of planning, and to know the operation of controls and gears in economy.

**(iii) Agriculture in the National Economy**

The scholars' knowledge should be comprehensive both at the macro-level and the micro-level. Agriculture in the National Economy includes the productivity trends, land use and crop pattern, agricultural inputs and methods and the role of land reforms in raising agricultural productivity and providing social justice. Besides these, the problems of organisation of rural credit, marketing and warehousing and the role of co-operation, community development and Panchayati Raj in the rural India are to be thoroughly comprehended. Similarly, the food problem and the impact of Five Year Plans on agriculture development should be properly integrated into his knowledge so that both the achievements and problems of agriculture in the national economy can be well noted.

### (iv) Indian Industries

Knowledge of Indian industries unfolds industrial pattern that was inherited by national government and the influence of the Five Year Plans in shaping the industrial pattern to suit the needs of a progressive economy. Discussion of large-scale enterprises and small-scale enterprises with specific industries and the problems of industrial finance and management is a basic requirement so that the scholar can have a comparative perspective of such enterprises.

### (v) Indian Labour

Thorough knowledge of Indian labour is essential to the economic scholars. The problem of unemployment, surplus labour and skill formation provides the scholar a broad view of the occupational distribution of Indian labour and the extent of maladjustment in its demand and supply in different sectors. Problems of industrial labour and its organisation, agricultural labour and labour policy are the reality of any economy and hence the scholar should be enriched with up-to-date knowledge as well as concern for labour problems.

### (vi) The Tertiary Sector in the Indian Economy

The Indian economy has a tertiary sector also. The tertiary sector in the Indian economy deals with the problems of transport and communications, the foreign trade of India, and its balance of payments position, the growth of Indian fiscal policy, the history of Indian currency, the role of commercial banks and the influence of the Reserve Bank of India (RBI) in developing and organized money market in India. Problems of Indian public finance are as important as other aspects of the tertiary sector.

## 2. RESEARCH METHODOLOGY

Apart from his knowledge of Indian economy as such which is his main area of research, the scholar should also have a thorough grounding in the research methodology which provides direction to the research as such. This includes thorough knowledge of sampling and designs, testing of hypothesis, multi-variate analysis, basic or fundamental ideas in linear programming, elements of input-output analysis, data base of the Indian economy, basic computer applications, as well as software packages. Such deep knowledge is essential as knowledge of statistics; software and hardware have become fundamental aspects of economic research.

## 3. SELECTED TOPICS IN ECONOMIC THEORY AND ECONOMIC POLICIES

Research scholars are expected to have deep insights into certain selected topics in economic theory and economic policies which include advanced topics in micro economics like managerial theories of the firm, theories of pricing (M.C. Pricing and Limit Pricing), game theory and applications. Similarly, in macro-economics the scholars are to be thorough with rational expectations, new macro-economics, endogenous growth models, etc.

Indian economic applications are not only relevant but also leave their imprints on the public, which are about economic reforms and poverty, second generation reforms, fiscal reforms, financial sector reforms, trade policy, WTO and India, etc. Selected topics in Indian agricultural sector include food security, ever green revolution, green banking, agri-business and agro-processing. Energy security includes oil crises and Indian economy, alternative energy sources and problems and prospects.

**Selected Topics**

Regional economic cooperation is of much significance in the Indian economy which includes trade blocks, and multi-lateral trade including SAARC, NAFTA, and European Union, etc.

India's population and environment is another important topic in economic theory and economic policies. Trends and variations in India's population size, and structure, demographic divide, sustainable development, SEZ, etc. are the scholar's food for thought. Nowadays we have realised the significance and importance of inclusive growth strategies which includes social exclusion and inclusive growth, Five Year Eleventh Plan and Social Sector Reforms, NREGS, etc.

**Sources of Latest Information**

The research scholar has to collect the latest information available from government publications. Published and unpublished sources, journals and articles by eminent economists and special editions of standard and widely recognized news papers provide authentic information. Also, internet and other sources are also available due to developments in the information technology, eminent scholars in the teaching profession, other research scholars and all others who are experts in the field of Indian economics and economic problems are the sources who can enrich the scholars' knowledge through academic interactions, suggestions and criticism for the improvement of the scholars knowledge and perspectives. The scholar should do systematic reference work. For example, in the case of Research Methodology, books by Goode and Hatt, M.H. Gopal, are of much value, whereas for statistics, books by Freund, Yates, Gupta and Kapoor, Asthana provide proper information. There are books by Kim, Schroeder, William Klecka which are written on particular statistical techniques. ISI Data-base and Demaris Digit Modelling provide the required information for research scholars. Similarly, there are good sources for selected topics in economic theory and economic policies. They include books by Mankiw Gregory both for Macro-economics and micro-economics, Edward Shapiro for macro economic analysis and so on. There are good many books on Indian economy by Ishwar Dhingra, Dutt and Sundaram, Mishra and Puri, Pratiyogita Darpan, etc. while Debraj Ray is generally recommended for Development economics. The scholar should also be familiar with the Eleventh Five Year Plan (2007) by Planning Commission.

**The One Year M.Phil. Programme**

The one-year M.Phil. programme was introduced at the instance of UGC some 30 years ago, with two components: course work and dissertation. In some Universities, the M.Phil. degree has become a pre-requisite for admission to the Ph.D. programme. The M.Phil. programme is suitable for scholars who can commit their life only for a shorter period of one year or so, as the Ph.D.

programme requires much longer time commitment of at least four years.

### Research Admission through Research Common Entrance Test (RCET)

Usually Universities admit candidates into M.Phil. or Ph.D. programmes through Research Common Entrance Test (RCET). This test consists of objective items related to the course content at the postgraduate level. Based on the ranks obtained by the candidates, and in accordance with the university/state government/UGC norms, the candidates with better performance get direct admission to the Ph.D. programme, while candidates slightly lower in performance get admission into M.Phil. programme only. Similarly, there are different patterns like whole-time M.Phil./Ph.D. programmes. Part-time M.Phil./Ph.D. programmes for employees who satisfy the minimum length of service usually 2-3 years for M.Phil., and 5 years for Ph.D. part time. Of course, fresh candidates without any experience are offered admissions into Full-time Programme only. We also have full-time Faculty Improvement Programme (FIP) for Teacher candidates who receive UGC Fellowships equal to their salaries and the sponsoring institutes are permitted to make temporary appointments.

### Integration of M.Phil. and Ph.D. Programmes

In his critique of the Report of the Fourth Review Committee (ICSSR, March 2007), Balakrishnan (2008) has argued for the integration of the M.Phil. and Ph.D. programmes. This suggestion is made with a view to saving the time of the research scholar aiming at a Ph.D. degree. If M.Phil. degree is not a pre-requisite to the Ph.D. admission, this suggestion becomes redundant.

### Continuation from M.Phil. to Ph.D. Programme

In some Universities, on successful completion of M.Phil programme, the candidate is permitted, usually after lapse of one month, to apply to the university authorities, through proper channel for conversion of his original M.Phil. registration into Ph.D. registration on the basis of the M.Phil. degree so that the candidate can save at least one year without waiting for any Research Common Entrance Test called RCET.

### Evalution of M.Phil./Ph.D. Programme (Theory)

In some Universities, both M.Phil. and Ph.D. scholars are required to take the M.Phil./Pre-Ph.D. Common Examination (written) after a period of 10 months from the date of admissions as per the syllabus of the course content. Classes are held for these courses. The schedule and the conduct of the examinations are done by the Director of Admissions. The Pre-Ph.D./M.Phil. Theory Common Examinations (written) consist of three papers as shown below:

In case the syllabus is given in Unit pattern, there will be 5 Questions each having two items a and b, and the candidate has to answer either a or b by internal choice. Even if the candidate answers both 'a' and 'b' he is given marks for one of them only, usually the better answer.

### M.Phil. Dissertation

For M.Phil. degree, the candidate has to submit a dissertation based on empirical work, of course under the supervision of the Research Guide or Research Director after one year in the case of full-time candidates and after two years in the case of part-time candidates. The dissertation is evaluated for 150 marks by both the internal examiner usually the Research Guide or Research Director and the external examiner independently. Further, the candidate has to undergo a viva-voce examination by the research committee consisting of the Research Director, Head of the Department and The Chairman of the P.G. Board of Studies. The candidate is evaluated for 50 marks based on his performance in the viva-voce examination. The total marks for 200, that is, 150 for the dissertation taking the average of the internal and external marks awarded to the candidate and the viva-voce marks out of 50 awarded by the Viva-Voce Committee.

| *Paper* | *Title* | *Nature* | *Marks* | *Time* | *No. of Questions* |
|---|---|---|---|---|---|
| Paper I | Research Methodology | Common to all | 100 | 3 Hours | Any 5 out of 10 |
| Paper II | Selected Topics in Economic Theory and Economic Policies | Common to all | 100 | 3 Hours | Any 5 out of 10 |
| Paper III | Specialisation | Each candidate to answer a paper on his topic | | | |

### Evaluating Performance: Social Relevance in Research

While evaluating performance, an important consideration is the issue of social relevance in research in economics in response to the changing economic environment globally and within the country or state. This issue of relevance in social science research was discussed in the late seventies at a seminar held at the Institute of Economic Growth, Delhi, where several leading economists in the country participated. That is why, usually the sociological factors in economic development and economic transition of India included in the course on 'Indian Economy'.

### Problems of M.Phil./Ph.D. Programmes

(1) It is true that with the proliferation of Universities over the past couple of decades, the average quality of M.Phil./Ph.D. dissertations seems to have deteriorated.

(2) During the past 10-15 years economists with good training at the M.A. level have been able to get lucrative jobs in the private sector, both academic and administrative cadres and some through campus interviews and the number of candidates seeking admission to the M.Phil./Ph.D. programmes has dwindled appreciably.

(3) Candidates are shunning the Institutions which insist on high standards for the dissertations. This reflects on the standards of the candidates.

(4) The ICSSR and even the UGC doctoral/M.Phil. Scholarships are not sufficiently attractive for the talented.

(5) With the retirement, the senior faculty getting away and younger generation seeking better venues, well trained economists are now in short supply both for teaching and research positions in the public sector.

(6) While economics as a discipline is witnessing rapid advances in several areas other than teaching, the quality of teaching in representative college/some University departments in India seems to have declined, along with general decline in education.

## Reasons for the Problems in M.Phil. and Ph.D. Programmes

*1. Quality decline*

The quality decline may be due to duplication of topics or work, lack of motivation on the part of the scholar and the Research Director, M.Phil. duration of one year may be too short while the Ph.D. thesis are submitted coinciding with the advertisement for selection of faculty and so on.

*2. Dwindling number seeking research admissions*

Apart from lucrative jobs for talented M.A. level economists in the private sector which is good in one way, fee-hike may be another reason not openly expressed by the candidates. Further candidates feel that research takes longer periods and hence they may become over-aged for the job market.

*3. Shunning the institutes which insist on high standards*

The Institutes which insist on high standards may think of starting their own P.G. Courses so that they can become a catchment area for talent, while the institutes which do not insist on high standards should improve their academic atmosphere, faculty, revise course structure, and teaching quality.

*4. Scholarships*

When the scholarship is not attractive, institutes can think of raising the scholarship which may be a financial burden, or improve their facilities, perks and other benefits including weightage to their prestigious institutes in job markets by building better academic image.

*5. Short supply of economists for teaching and research*

It is a fact that recruitments are not made regularly while retirements are made as per the age of superannuation without raising the age of retirement. Hence timely recruitment should be undertaken and retired teachers' services may be utilised for a shorter period of two years to five years or as long as their health permits. This can be done on contractive basis and consolidated honorarium.

6. *Decline in the quality of teaching*

The quality of teaching can be improved by deputing the junior faculty members to orientation and refresher programmes offered by UGC Academic Staff Colleges, professional bodies, apex organisations or University Economics departments can organize such courses with UGC or other funding agencies.

## Research in Economics by the Teaching Faculty in Colleges and Universities

While the teaching faculty in a small proportion of higher education in economics (in colleges and universities) has produced research output of good quality in sufficient amount, the total research output of quality in the higher education sector seems to have fallen short of expectations.

Some of the factors responsible for insufficient good research output are:

(i) Heavy teaching loads,
(ii) Inadequate research facilities,
(iii) Unsatisfactory prior training,
(iv) Weak standards of accountability, and
(v) Absence of research culture in some instances.

Some of these points have been identified by Anita Mehta as well.

## Post-doctoral Fellowships

Post-doctoral Fellowship Scheme is meant to upgrade the analytical skills of young economists who earned their Ph.D. degrees in India. During 1989-97, NIPEP—Ford Post-doctoral Fellowship Scheme enabled 38 Indian economists under 40 years to spend one year in Universities of their choice in the U.S. or the U.K. for sharpening their skills under the guidance of senior professors. I.G. Patel who evaluated the scheme observed that the scheme served useful academic purpose. Almost all these scholars have subsequently won laurels in the profession.

## Flexible Schemes for Research

Recently IGIDR has introduced a Ph.D. programme for talented external candidates, requiring one year of course work and one more year of residence. Flexible schemes of this type of academically well endowed institutions are very much desirable.

IGIDR has also offered facilities for Ph.D. degree holders of other institutions to pursue post-doctoral research under the guidance of IGIDR faculty.

### Promoting Multi-disciplinary Research

Promoting multi-disciplinary research has always been a desirable goal in social science research. Several research institutions in the country have on their faculty scholars from different disciplines, e.g. Sociology, Political Science, Demography and Geography, apart from Economics. But, interactions among different disciplines and research output from collaborative effort between scholars from different disciplines, if any, has seldom been documented and evaluated.

For example, research in the field of Economics of Education may be undertaken by scholars from economics department with a postgraduate degree in Education and aptitude for education or by scholars from Education with a postgraduate degree in Economics and interest in economic aspects. Similarly, collaborative research can be undertaken by economists from different universities and institutes.

### Problems in Research Careers

Anita Mehta's comment (*EPW*, October 11, 2008) on Pushpa Bhargava's endorsement of the role of autonomous research institutes (*EPW*, August 2, 2008) as opposed to Gautam R. Desiraju's opinion that the creation of such institutes was a singular blunder (*EPW*, June 14, 2008) holds that while the real backbone of our education is to be found within the traditional University system, the faculty at research institutions need more support in doing pure research.

Anita Mehta said:

> ".......those who manage to perform well in most of our Research Institutions are usually fighting enormous battles just to survive; especially if they are not playing politics as well."

Though Anita Mehta's observations are on 'Science

Research in India', they apply to research in any discipline including Economics. Hence, her observations may be presented in a detailed manner.

Further Mehta said:

> "Research Careers are typically not well-rewarded and, in today's society, not particularly well respected; added to this is the value not added of the physical and mental surroundings they have to work in. While all of this is true of Universities as well, the "autonomous" nature of most Research Institutes sets them apart from the democracy of most Universities; but suffice it to say that merit is usually the first casuality of politics. The fact that scientists whose spirits might have been repeatedly broken by political manoeuvres are still able to be productive is nothing short of a miracle; they need to be supported, and not discouraged. Closing down Research Institutes, or modifying them out of all recognition, is thus not a fair solution—at least not for the active researchers within them."

## CONCLUSIONS

The Report of the Fourth Review Committee, while giving credit to the ICSSR for creating and supporting 27 social science research institutes in different parts of the country with state governments as partners has expressed its concern that 'the impact of social science research has fallen short of expectations'. Both Anita Mehta and Review Committee have identified similar factors responsible for insufficient good research output, like: heavy teaching work, inadequate facilities, unsatisfactory training, and weak standards of accountability and absence of research culture.

### Recommendations of the Fourth Review Committee Report

The Report has made the following recommendations:

(i) Greater autonomy of ICSSR,
(ii) Steep increase in funding,
(iii) The constitution of a new Academy of Social Science that would replace the ICSSR.

As observed by Anita Mehta (2008), "A little respect for the freedom of choice of individuals who have chosen to train long years, and adjured the lure of more lucrative professions, for the love of the intellectual life and inherent liberties will surely go a long way."

## REFERENCES

Bhargava, Pushpa M. (2008), "On the Organisation of Science Research in India", *Economic and Political Weekly*, Mumbai, August 2.

Datt, Ruddar and Sundaram, K.P.M. (2001), Indian Economy, S. Chand & Company Ltd., New Delhi.

Desiraju, Gautam R. (2008), "Science Education and Research in India", *Economic and Political Weekly*, Mumbai, June 14.

Mehta, Anita (2008), "Science Research in India: Universities, Research Institutes and Everything in-between", *Economic and Political Weekly*, Mumbai, October 11.

# Globalisation and Quality Education

## How can this be Ensured?

ANUP K. MISHRA, P.K. SEN AND RAJ KISHOR PANDEY

### INTRODUCTION

Globalisation, over the years, is transforming the lives of the people. Not only the national economies but also the national cultures are globalising. Today, globalisation means much more than mere opening up of economies and competition. In fact, globalisation has acquired much wider concept. It is now more understood as 'Functioning on a Planetary Scale on Real Time', meaning that 'information is exchanged or communicated as it is produced'.

Today Globalisation means much more than opening up of economies and competition. It is also now the 'functioning on a planetary scale on real time', in the sense that information is exchanged or communicated as it is produced.

There are wide diversity of factors and forces that are attributing to the after-effects of globalisation. In essence, it is how economic growth potentials, work force requirements, and the work-market that are getting reoriented, as ultimately they not only create conditions but also determines the state of socio-economic development.

Under the new global economic climate, the ability to create such conditions will depend increasingly on the way the government culture the education system. It is so because, knowledge is the most highly valued commodity in the global economy, and the nations have little choice but to increase their investment in education. The call of the day is not merely quantity but the quality of education. This is more so because the problem today is not merely of employment but more of employability.

## CONCEPTUAL BACKGROUND

### Globalisation

Acceptance of such concept of globalisation in conjunction with Information Technology, one then can visualize changing format of national economy and social culture, as there is vast change in the knowledge, attitude and work culture of the fellow citizens. No society or population can remain immune to the effects of such change. It will perhaps be more correct to state that it is changing the very basics and essentials of human relations and social life.

### Transmission of Knowledge

In the present day, movement of capital depends upon information, communication and transmission of knowledge in the global market. As knowledge is easily transmittable, it has become fundamentally supporting to Globalisation.

This brings us two hypotheses:

(i) The first proposition is that, Globalisation has a reflective effect on Education. For the reason that knowledge is fundamental to Globalisation, Globalisation in turn, should also have a reflective impact on the Transmission of knowledge.
However, there are arguments against this. There are evidences where Globalisation has failed to access local or region-specific culture-influenced knowledge production and transmission.

(ii) This brings us to the second preposition that despite of nations involved in Globalisation and Information Technology, education appears to have changed little in most countries at the classroom level. Further than occasionally using computers in classrooms, teaching methods and academic curricula remains unaffected and unaltered. In addition, decentralisation of educational administration and finance seems to have little or no impact on educational delivery in classrooms.

Now the question is can we really draw the clear line of cut-off between the two prepositions, is not, is such impact on transitional stage? Inclusion of such event brings three propositions, namely:

(1) Globalisation is having a profound impact on Education at national, regional and even local levels, reintegrating the individuals into the new society based on information and knowledge.
(2) As the opposite case, Globalisation is having a little impact on Education at national, regional and even local levels.
(3) Globalisation is having an increasing impact on Education at national level; yet, the regional and even local levels are still far away from its vaccination.

## MATRIX OF THE PROBLEM

### (A) Impact of Globalisation on Education

With the presumption that Globalisation is having an increasing impact on Education, such impact can be seen as:

#### *(i) The Changes in the Labour Markets and Education Systems*

With the newer demand for workforces capable of production of competitive goods with a high level of skill-content, such impact is clearly on the organisation of work as well as on very nature of work people do.

#### *(ii) Work Flexibility in the Labour Markets and Education Systems*

Work in the labour market is becoming more flexible. Increasingly, workers now have more options to change their kinds of jobs and their jobs now tend to be more multitasked.

Such flexibility in the job market demands pressure to increase not only the average level of education and higher education, but also for technical education for higher skills.

*(iii) Rising Pay-off to Higher and Technical Education*

The pay-off to levels of higher education along with technical education is fast increasing. Worldwide, there is a clear shift towards Skill-Intensive Products and Knowledge-oriented Markets.

Rising relative incomes for higher educated and skill oriented labour, in turn, increases the demand for university education as well as of technical education.

*(iv) Pressure to Increase Spending on Higher and Technical Education*

Along with the increases in the demand for university and technical education, there is now the pressure to increase spending on Higher and Technical Education to generate a more educated labour force.

However, in most of the developing countries, guaranteeing of the demand for additional resources for higher and technical universities is coupled with the role of both government and private sector.

*(v) The Consequential Decentralisation and Privatisation of Education System*

In order to meet the initial increasing pressure to increase spending on Higher and Technical Education to generate a more educated labour force, decentralisation and privatisation of education system seems to be the immediate alternative with the governments.

In this regard, it is argued that decentralisation and privatisation of education system is the most effective strategy for ensuring quality and flexibility in the supply of a more educated labour force in a globalised economy. In other words, the pressure to supply more educated and more technical labourforce appear to have a private-sector bias.

*(vi) The Quality of National Education*

The ultimate goal to invest more and more in human resources and in quality education and technical training at all levels is translated with increased privatisation and marketisation of education financing and management. Consequently, there lies the wider implication of testing of education quality and the real effect of technological change.

*(vii) Information Technology and the Quality of Education*

The planetary role of Information technology to extend Quality education at lower cost is vital to the development of globalised labour market. However, the extent of its effectiveness differs from country to country.

The capacity of globalisation to have profound impact on the transmission of knowledge on the local and regional levels is often hurdled by age long rigid and deep-rooted culture-influenced knowledge. Beyond occasionally, using computers in classrooms, the teaching methods and national curricula remains largely unchanged.

However, there seems to be a common agreement to the need that the fundamental role of educational institutions should not only be to transmit skills needed in the global economy, but also to effect the future of the individuals at the local, regional and national level.

*(viii) Cultural Transformation Through New Meaning and Value of Knowledge*

As and when individuals are exposed to and adopt higher global knowledge to enable them to be a stronger force in the labour market, there is inculcation of new meaning and value of life. Such cultural transformation seems to be inevitable.

However, with such globalisation, there lies the danger of many groups to be marginalised by the market values of this culture. Such groups tussle against globalised market forces that tend to threaten their traditional culture, and thus are anti-market. This there from, amount to an intellectual struggle (towards inclusive growth) over the globalised meaning and value of knowledge.

## IMPACT OF GLOBALISATION ON EMPLOYMENT

### Market Interdependence and Segmentation

In the context of globalisation and labour market, the foremost question arises: Is Labour also globalised? The answer is probably no. Such judgment is because of the fact that today there is a huge supply of highly skilled and educated workers in the countries like India and China. They can meet the needs of global organisations at a comparatively lower wage than that say in America.

Thus, even if labours do not circulate globally to the same extent as money and goods do, there is surely an increased interdependence of labour market. Such interdependence is then characterized by hierarchical segmentation of labour cutting across the global boundaries. Interdependence and segmentation of labour market has its own advantage and disadvantage for the domestic economy.

### Globalisation of Skills and the Left-Out Unskilled

As labour does not circulate globally, there has been consequent increase in the interdependence of labour markets. However, while the skilled workers are benefited from the process, the unskilled workers lost out in the competition. Further, with the fall in demand of unskilled workers, their wages also decline.

### The Danger of Reducing Demand for Unskilled

Over the recent years, one major adverse effect of globalisation is marked with reducing demand for unskilled labour. More sufferers are those university graduates who are obtaining traditional degrees (like, simply B.A. or M.A.). There is a general tendency to associate this with effects of globalisation and advent of new technology.

More important is, perhaps, the nation's educational policies. The governments incorporating the policy of Globalisation cannot overlook the fact that globalisation and new technology are truly knowledge-intensive; the evolved labour markets are much knowledge-intensive, flexible, disaggregate and individualised. These strategic features should occupy its vital importance in the education policy of such nation.

### Individualizing Work Task and Differentiating Workers

Markably, the term 'job' might not mean the same thing in the future as it does today. This is so because globalisation is fast changing the nature and type of job. Amidst competition, the factors like cost and productivity have become much important. As a way out, this thereby has compelled the corporate world to design work-differentiation and individualizing work tasks.

However, the effect of individualisation and differentiation, separating workers from their full-time traditional jobs, has proved to be quite dangerous. They are now as 'permanently temporary' as the work itself.

### Information Technology and Employment

Information Technology and employment growth has experienced most worldwide positive growth during 1980s and 1990s especially in USA. In contrast, during the'90s, there was no relation between the intensity of use of information technology and the rate of unemployment in Spain. Further, lower use of technology in Spain (as compared to France) is marked with higher unemployment rate (than in France).

## EVALUATION OF THE PRESENT STATUS OF LEVEL OF EDUCATION

The following two statements are based on the 61st round of NSS, depicting:

(1) levels of education at different MPCE levels; and
(2) levels of Vocational training at different are groups.

### Statement I

Number of non-literates and number of educated persons per 1000 persons of age 15 years and above for each monthly per-capita consumer expenditure (MPCE) class during 2004-05 (all-India)

| MPCE | MALE | MALE | FEMALE | FEMALE | PERSON | PERSON |
|---|---|---|---|---|---|---|
| Class (Rs.) | Not literate | Educated | Not literate | Educated | Not literate | Educated |
| (1) | (2) | (3) | (4) | (5) | (6) | (7) |
| | | | Rural | | | |
| less than 235 | 573 | 54 | 799 | 19 | 692 | 36 |
| 235-270 | 505 | 53 | 778 | 17 | 648 | 34 |
| 270-320 | 458 | 93 | 755 | 31 | 609 | 61 |
| 320-365 | 441 | 101 | 715 | 35 | 581 | 68 |
| 365-410 | 384 | 131 | 668 | 45 | 527 | 87 |
| 410-455 | 372 | 152 | 648 | 61 | 509 | 106 |
| 455-510 | 340 | 160 | 614 | 66 | 477 | 113 |
| 510-580 | 290 | 207 | 571 | 90 | 429 | 150 |
| 580-690 | 257 | 249 | 517 | 122 | 385 | 187 |
| 690-890 | 214 | 306 | 454 | 168 | 332 | 237 |
| 890-1155 | 169 | 401 | 373 | 240 | 267 | 323 |
| 1155 & above | 102 | 542 | 256 | 365 | 176 | 457 |
| All classes | 320 | 211 | 585 | 102 | 452 | 156 |

| | | | Urban | | | |
|---|---|---|---|---|---|---|
| less than 335 | 376 | 121 | 632 | 65 | 505 | 92 |
| 335-395 | 314 | 167 | 570 | 82 | 445 | 124 |
| 395-485 | 267 | 196 | 515 | 102 | 390 | 150 |
| 485-580 | 203 | 256 | 427 | 159 | 314 | 207 |
| 580-675 | 170 | 319 | 373 | 193 | 269 | 257 |
| 675-790 | 109 | 386 | 296 | 259 | 199 | 325 |
| 790-930 | 97 | 463 | 244 | 332 | 166 | 402 |
| 930-1100 | 74 | 526 | 201 | 386 | 134 | 460 |
| 1100-1380 | 52 | 634 | 138 | 505 | 92 | 574 |
| 1380-1880 | 25 | 733 | 103 | 601 | 61 | 672 |
| 1880-2540 | 16 | 825 | 74 | 702 | 43 | 767 |
| 2540 & above | 11 | 905 | 27 | 825 | 18 | 866 |
| All classes | 121 | 483 | 279 | 356 | 196 | 422 |

**Statement 2**

Per 1000 distribution of persons of age 15-29 years by vocational training received/being received for each age group (all-India)

| Age group (years) | Vocational training | No vocational training | Total (incl. n.r.) | % with no vocational training |
|---|---|---|---|---|
| (1) | (2) | (3) | (4) | (5) |
| | | **Rural male** | | |
| 15-19 | 81 | 909 | 1000 | 90.9 |
| 20-24 | 142 | 850 | 1000 | 85.0 |
| 15-24 | 108 | 883 | 1000 | 88.3 |
| 25-29 | 150 | 842 | 1000 | 84.2 |
| All (15-29) | 120 | 871 | 1000 | 87.1 |
| | | | | |
| | | **Rural female** | | |
| 15-19 | 69 | 921 | 1000 | 92.1 |
| 20-24 | 84 | 909 | 1000 | 90.9 |
| 15-24 | 77 | 915 | 1000 | 91.5 |
| 25-29 | 85 | 898 | 1000 | 89.8 |
| All (15-29) | 79 | 910 | 1000 | **91.0** |
| | | | | |
| | | **Rural person** | | |
| 15-19 | 76 | 914 | 1000 | 91.4 |
| 20-24 | 112 | 880 | 1000 | 88.0 |
| 15-24 | 93 | 898 | 1000 | 89.8 |
| 25-29 | 117 | 871 | 1000 | 87.1 |
| All (15-29) | 100 | 890 | 1000 | **89.0** |
| | | | | |
| | | **Urban male** | | |
| 15-19 | 107 | 887 | 1000 | 88.7 |
| 20-24 | 214 | 783 | 1000 | 78.3 |
| 15-24 | 159 | 837 | 1000 | 83.7 |
| 25-29 | 223 | 771 | 1000 | 77.1 |
| All (15-29) | 178 | 817 | 1000 | 81.7 |

| Urban female | | | | |
|---|---|---|---|---|
| 15-19 | 78 | 915 | 1000 | 91.5 |
| 20-24 | 140 | 856 | 1000 | 85.6 |
| 15-24 | 109 | 885 | 1000 | 88.5 |
| 25-29 | 123 | 870 | 1000 | 87.0 |
| All (15-29) | 113 | 881 | 1000 | **88.1** |
| Urban person | | | | |
| 15-19 | 94 | 900 | 1000 | 90.0 |
| 20-24 | 179 | 817 | 1000 | 81.7 |
| 15-24 | 136 | 859 | 1000 | 85.9 |
| 25-29 | 175 | 818 | 1000 | 81.8 |
| All (15-29) | 148 | 847 | 1000 | **84.7** |

Based on the data of these two NSS-statements, some correlations and Time trends are drawn and the results are presented over the Tables 1 to 3.

RESULT TABLE I

**Correlation Coefficients between Monthly Per-capita Consumer Expenditure (MPCE) Class and Levels of Education**

| CORRELATION : MPCE Vs. Edıcation Level | | | |
|---|---|---|---|
| Rural | | | |
| | Male | Not Literate | - 0.933 |
| | | Literate | 0.998 |
| | Female | Not Literate | -0.982 |
| | | Literate | 0.995 |
| | Person | Not Literate | -0.963 |
| | | Literate | 0.998 |
| Urban | | | |
| | Male | Not Literate | - 0.794 |
| | | Literate | 0.950 |
| | Female | Not Literate | - 0.866 |
| | | Literate | 0.972 |
| | Person | Not Literate | -0.837 |
| | | **Literate** | **0.960** |

## Result Table 2

### Trend Values of Literates and Not Literates

| TREND VALUES | | |
|---|---|---|
| **RURAL NOT LITERATE** | | **URBAN NOT LITERATE** |
| **Female** | y = - 45.59 x + 892.03 | y = - 56x + 664 |
| | R2 = 0.95 | R2 = 0.9869 |
| | | |
| **Male** | y = - [illegible]8.98 x + 595.42 | y = - 33.028x + 357.52 |
| | R2 = 0.99 | R2 = 0.9339 |
| | | |
| **Person** | y = - 43.18 x + 750.02 | y = - 44.846x + 511.17 |
| | R2 = 0.77 | R2 = 0.9699 |
| | | |
| **RURAL LITERATE** | | **URBAN LITERATE** |
| **Female** | y = 25.689x - 62.061 | y = 69.283x - 99.424 |
| | R2 = 0.768 | R2 = 0.9506 |
| | | |
| **Male** | y = 38.346x - 45.167 | y = 73.052x - 13.924 |
| | R2 = 0.8629 | R2 = 0.9811 |
| | | |
| **Person** | y = 32.36x - 55.424 | y = 71.594x - 57.364 |
| | R2 = 0.8264 | R2 = 0.9698 |

## Result Table 3

### Trend Values of Vocational and No Vocational Trainings

| Rural male | | |
|---|---|---|
| | Vocational | y = 17.3 x + 77 |
| | | $R^2 = 0.4908$ |
| | | |
| | No Vocational | y =- 16.8 x + 913 |
| | | $R^2 = 0.4917$ |
| Rural female | | |
| | Vocational | y = 4.1x + 68.5 |
| | | $R^2 = 0.5102$ |
| | | |
| | No Vocational | y =- 6.3x + 926.5 |
| | | $R^2 = 0.6873$ |

| | | |
|---|---|---|
| Rural person | | |
| | Vocational | y = 10.4x + 73. |
| | | $R^2 = 0.5116$ |
| | | |
| | No Vocational | y =-11.1x + 918.5 |
| | | $R^2 = 0.5607$ |
| | | |
| Urban male | | |
| | Vocational | y = 29.3x + 102.5 |
| | | $R^2 = 0.4932$ |
| | | |
| | No Vocational | y =-29.4x + 893 |
| | | $R^2 = 0.5057$ |
| Urban female | | |
| | Vocational | y = 10.4x + 86.5 |
| | | $R^2 = 0.2614$ |
| | | |
| | No Voctional | y =-10.6x + 908 |
| | | $R^2 = 0.2931$ |
| Urban person | | |
| | Vocational | y = 20x + 96 |
| | | $R^2 = 0.4225$ |
| | | |
| | No Vocational | y =-20.4x + 899.5 |
| | | $R^2 = 0.4441$ |

- Based on the Result Table 1, clearly we find, with the rise in monthly per-capita consumer expenditure (MPCE) class, there have been corresponding fall in illiteracy levels (both rural and urban). As a corollary, with rise in MPCE, the level of literacy is very high. This confirms that with the dynamic income, the consumer expenditure as an important factor towards the level of literacy in the country. This is also validated by the NSS data (Statement-1), where the highest frequencies of 'not literate' are in the lowest MPCE slab, and the highest frequencies of 'literate' are in the highest MPCE slab.
- In as much as the trends of 'not literates' are concerned, all are marked with falling trends. That is, the levels of illiterates (both female and male in both rural and urban) are reducing (Result Table-2). It is quite appealing to mark the fall in the female illiteracy levels (both rural and urban) are greater than the fall in male.

- With the rising 'age-groups', the trends of 'vocational' and 'no vocational' training are presented in the Result Table 3. The markable features are:
  - (i) Fall in 'no vocational training' are greater for male than female in both rural and urban sectors.
  - (ii) Fall in 'no vocational training' of urban person is almost double than rural person.
  - (iii) Clearly, thus, there lies the need to work more towards higher 'vocational training' not only for female but also specially for both male and female in the rural sector.

## ENSURING THE NEED OF QUALITY EDUCATION: THE WAY-OUT

### Investment Patterns in National Education Policies

Thus, interdependence and segmentation of labour market has meaningful bearing for national educational planners, especially in terms of higher and technical education.

However, education in general and higher education in particular are historically linked with inherent national objectives of promoting national culture and national heritage. Yet, the fact also remains that today education investment policies are also highly internationalised to meet the global market needs. Thus, the challenge is to get the typical blend of traditional and modern education policy measures, as the importance of each cannot be just ignored or belittled. From this perspective, one can easily see the relative roles of Public sector and Private sector investments in the education sector.

### Rates of Return of Investments in Education

With the rising global demand for higher level skills, the rate of returns to investment in higher education (relative to the pay-offs to investing in primary and secondary schooling) is pushing up. Rates of return to higher levels of education are also pushed up by government's structural adjustment policies. All these tend to favour those with higher skill levels. However, such rates of returns may differ in absolute and relative terms.

The case is, whether investments in higher education should purely be judged by its rates of return. The answer to this is encircled by the policy objectives of national policy. Such policies are generally multi-dimensional and cannot be singled out.

### The Social Implications

Globalisation also does have social implications of higher rates of return to higher education. In general, it is marked that majority of those having higher social class background, get to higher levels of education. Such higher socio-economic status (SES) students have greater access to better schools. As an outcome, lower SES students get a lower stake (in both private and public system school).

As an alternative, in Brazil, Chile, Colombia, Malaysia and even in India, commercial and private academic institutions have almost become 'Diploma Mills', serving students from lower SES, despite of the fact that they get generally lower return than those from well recognized public and private universities.

Based on the above policy implications, in the event of globalisation, the need for quality education is being re-conceptualised through the flow-chart.

## GLOBALISATION AND QUALITY EDUCATION: THE FLOW CHART

Globalisation means much more than mere opening up of economies and competition. It is now more empathised as 'Functioning on a Planetary Scale on Real Time'. In essence, globalisation is not strictly surrounded by trade and investments, nor it is the percentage of national economy that is national, but it is also more in a new approach of consideration on the subject of economic and social liberty and occasion. In brief, there is re-conceptualisation of 'world'.

Among the other factors of production, as labour do not seem to be much globalise, rather there is increased interdependence of labour markets, globalisation is having real impact on organisation of work and on the nature of the work people do.

**Globalisation and Quality Education**
**The Flow Chart**

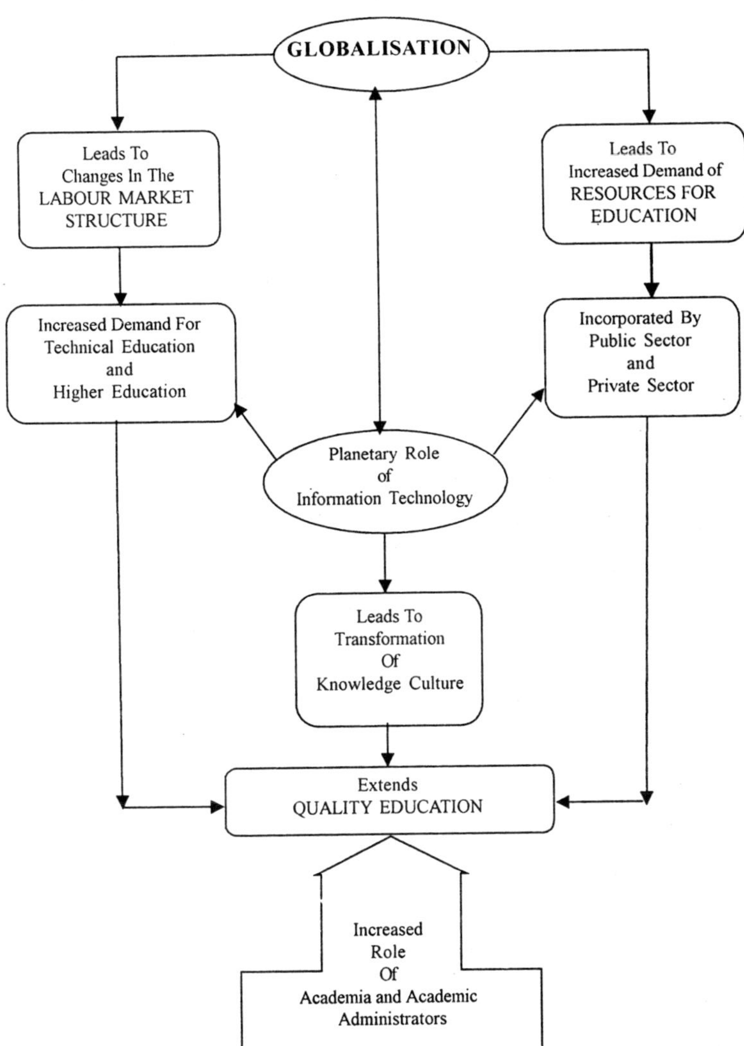


This leads to:

(a) Changes in the Labour Market Structure.
(b) Increased demand for Resources for Education.

(i) The changes in the Labour Market structure is due to the increased demand for both Technical education and Higher education, which is the skill content of the new global demand of labour market.

(ii) Simultaneously, as the Increased Demand for Resources for Education, is hostile to the expansion of the role of the public sector, we can see the vast inflow of privatisation in the education sector.

(iii) Thus, while on one hand, there is vast increase of demand for technical and higher education, on the other hand, there is increased role of private sector to meet this increased demand.

(iv) Under this scenario of globalisation, there is the Planetary Role of Information technology. With the use of Information and Communication Technology, it has not only change the dynamics of higher and technical education, but also has removed the age long barriers which had been causing the under growth in this sector.

(v) As the most important imprecation, one may mark a speedy Transformation of Knowledge Culture that ultimately severs the goal of increased Quality Education.

(vi) Finally, in order to Ensure Quality Education, there is the increased Role Of Academia and Academic Administrators.

## References

1. As per the 61st round of NSS:

* *About 73 per cent of the households belonged to rural India and these accounted for nearly 75 per cent of the total population.*
* In about 26 per cent of the households in the rural areas and about 8 per cent those in the urban areas, there was not a single member of age 15 years or above who could read and write a simple message with understanding.
* About 50 per cent of the rural households and about 20 per cent of the urban had no literate among the female members of age 15 years and above.
* Among the major States, the proportion of households with no literate among the members of age 15 years and above was found to be the lowest in Kerala (3 per cent) and the highest

in Bihar (38 per cent) in the rural areas. In the urban areas, it was found to be the lowest again in Kerala (1 per cent) and the highest in Rajasthan (16 per cent) followed by Bihar (15 per cent) and West Bengal (14 per cent).

* In India, the literacy rate was 64 per cent during 2004-05. The literacy rate was 55 per cent in the rural areas and 75 per cent in the urban areas. About 64 per cent of rural males and 45 per cent of rural females were literate. The literacy rates among their urban counterparts were much higher at 81 per cent and 69 per cent, respectively.
* In the rural areas of the major States, the literacy was the highest in Kerala (83 per cent) and the lowest in Bihar (44 per cent). On the other hand, in the urban areas of the major States, the literacy rate was the highest in Kerala (85 per cent) and the lowest in Rajasthan (64 per cent).
* The proportion of non-literates was found to be the highest in the bottom monthly per capita expenditure (MPCE) class and it decreased gradually as the MPCE increased.
* The proportion of the educated (i.e., those with level of general education secondary and above including diploma/certificate course) was found to be the lowest in the bottom MPCE class in the urban areas and the same was the case in the two bottom MPCE classes in the rural areas.
* Among persons of age 15 years and above, only 2 per cent had technical degrees or diplomas or certificates. The proportion was only 1 per cent in the rural areas and 5 per cent in the urban NSS Report No. 517: Status of Education and Vocational Training in India, 2004-05.

2. The Highlights of the 61st round of NSS:
   * About 50 per cent of people in the age group 5-29 years were currently attending educational institution. It was a little higher for males (53 per cent) than for females (46 per cent).
   * Among the major States, the current attendance rate for the age group 5-29 years was the highest in Himachal Pradesh (60 per cent) and the lowest in Orissa (42 per cent).
   * Government institutions accounted for 63 per cent of all students (i.e., those who were currently attending), followed by private unaided institutions (17 per cent), private aided institutions (14 per cent) and local body institutions (only 6 per cent).
   * Among males (5-29 years) who were currently not attending any educational institution, about 55 per cent reported the reason 'to supplement household income' for not attending. The reason 'to attend domestic chores' was reported by 30 per cent of females who were currently not attending any educational institution.
   * Among persons of age 15-29 years, about 2 per cent reported to have received formal vocational training and another 8 per cent reported to have received non-formal vocational training.

* Among the persons (15-29 years) who received formal vocational training, the most demanded field of training was 'computer trades' and around 31 per cent received such training.
* The Industrial Training Institutes (ITIs)/Industrial Training Centres (ITCs) played a major role in providing formal vocational training. About 20 per cent received formal vocational training from ITIs/ITCs.

# A Comparative Study of Teaching and Research in Economics and other Courses

GANGADHAR V. KAYANDE PATIL AND RAKESH S. PATIL

## INTRODUCTION: DATA AND SAMPLE

The data for the study were taken from the various colleges which are affiliated with University of Pune imparting the education in Undergraduate and Post Graduate in Economics as well as other Courses. The survey administered to faculty members was remarkably detailed and took almost an hour to complete. The questionnaire prepared for the survey and distributed to the various colleges. The weighted response rate was 83 percent. The focus of this study is on faculty preferences toward teaching and research in economics and other comparable Courses. We restricted the data set in three ways to make meaningful comparisons among similar types of faculty members.

Our analysis was first limited to faculty members in economics and seven other Courses or fields of study that focused on science. Faculty members in the arts and humanities were excluded from our analysis. The seven other Courses or fields of study were: (i) Social Sciences, (ii) Biological Sciences, (iii) Physical Sciences, (iv) Mathematics and Statistics, (v) Computer Science, (vi) Engineering, and (vii) Business Management.

The institutes considered for the survey other than research Institute. Because of many of the faculty members at these types of institutions typically have responsibilities for teaching and research as a condition of their employment. As a result, these faculty members must choose between teaching and research in their work allocation, and thus are likely to have opinions on this teaching and research trade-off in employment duties.

We limited the sample in a third way to those faculty members who reported being a Professor (Assistant Professor, Reader, Associate Professor) because these faculty members typically both teach and do research. Faculty members with appointments as lecturer, research associate, or some other title were omitted from the analysis because they typically do not have joint responsibilities for teaching and research.

The basic demographic characteristics of economics professors at research universities are similar to professors in other scientific Courses or fields. The great majority of faculty members in all Courses are male (88 percent in economics and 81 percent in the other Courses). Physical Sciences, Engineering, and Mathematics and Statistics have higher proportions of male professors than does economics, but Social Sciences, Biological sciences, and Business have a smaller proportion. Each Course or field is overwhelmingly while with economics and the Physical Sciences topping the list at 90 percent, and mathematics/Statistics and Engineering setting the lower bound at about 75 to 77 percent. Economics professors have an average age of 49, but there is only limited variation in age across Courses. The youngest professors are typically found in Computer Science and the oldest in the Physical Sciences. There are longevity characteristics of professors that are worth-noting to describe the sample. On average, economics professors have been teaching in higher education for 20.5 years, and they have held their current job for about 14.5 years. Economics professors have been teaching longer than professors in all other Courses (average: 17.6) except Mathematics and Statistics (21.3), and they have held their current position longer than professors in other Courses except for professors of Mathematics and Statistics or professors in the Physical Sciences.

## II. TEACHING AND RESEARCH PRODUCTION

The average teaching load is similar across all Courses. Economics professors in research universities teach two classes per semester on average, which is lower than the average teaching load in the Biological Sciences (2.2), Social Sciences (2.3), Computer Science (2.3), or Business (2.5). Professors in the Physical Sciences and in Engineering teach the same average number of classes as economics professors. The total seven of the eight Courses about two-thirds (65 percent) of the teaching is in undergraduate classes, and the other third is in graduate classes. The only exception is in the Biological sciences, where professors provide less undergraduate instruction (41 percent) and more graduate instruction (59 percent). Economics professors teach fewer classes, so it would be expected that they would most likely teach fewer students than most other Courses. In fact, economics professors teach about 11 fewer students each semester on average than do professors in the other Courses. Only professors in Computer Science and Mathematics and Statistics report teaching smaller number of students, but in both cases their teaching load is slightly higher. Also, in the case of Engineering and the Physical Sciences, where professors had the exact same teaching load as economics professors, the professors in these two Courses report teaching substantially more students on average than do economics professors (23 more in Engineering and 17 more in the Physical Sciences). Thus, there is no basic quantitative evidence that the teaching load of economics professors is heavier than that of professors in other Science Courses at research institutions. In fact, a case can be made that the teaching load of economics professors is slightly less in terms of classes taught and the number of students taught relative to most other Science Courses. One measure of research output of professors is the total number of articles published in refereed journals. On this outcome measure, economics professors are about in the middle of the distribution when compared with other professors in the sciences. The average number of refereed journal articles is much greater among professors in the Physical Sciences (59), the Biological Sciences (50), and also in Engineering (41). The journal output of economics professors (26) is most similar to those professors in the other Social Sciences. Only professors in Business and

Computer Science report fewer journal publications (16 and 20, respectively) over a career. A similar placement in the distribution also holds when comparing economics professors with other professors based on recent output. Economics professors averaged about seven refereed journal articles over the most recent two-year period covered by the survey, which is only one more publication than that for professors in the Social Sciences. Professors in the physical and Biological Sciences and in Engineering also showed the greatest rates of publication in recent-year comparisons.

TABLE I

**Teaching and Research Production**

| Sr. No. | Course/field | Teaching | | Research | |
|---|---|---|---|---|---|
| | | Classes No. | Student No. | Total | Recent |
| 1. | Economics | 2.0 | 78 | 26 | 7 |
| 2. | Other Courses | 2.2 | 85 | 40 | 8 |
| (i) | Social Science | 2.3 | 2.3 | 89 | 28 |
| (ii) | Biological Sciences | 2.2 | 101 | 50 | 10 |
| iii) | Physical Sciences | 2.0 | 95 | 59 | 11 |
| (iv) | Mathematics/Statistics | 2.1 | 66 | 33 | 8 |
| (v) | Computer Sciences | 2.3 | 75 | 20 | 6 |
| (vi) | Engineering | 2.0 | 101 | 41 | 10 |
| (vii) | Business Management | 2.5 | 97 | 16 | 4 |

There are differences in journal publishing across Courses that are affected by the number of journals in a Course, article length, the propensity to co-author, the distribution of professors by rank, and other factors. For example, professors in the physical and Biological sciences, and Engineering, probably produce more articles because they tend to be shorter in length and the work is more likely to be conducted by research teams. Professors in Business and Computer Science probably publish less because these two fields have a smaller fraction of fully promoted professors (19 percent for each) than does economics (46 percent) or the other Courses (39 percent). Counts of journal articles also provide no indication of quality. Nevertheless, there is nothing in the quantitative measure of research output that suggests that economics professors are more productive than other science-oriented professors, and an argument could be made that they are less productive in research relative to some Science Courses.

## III. ACTUAL AND PREFERRED USES OF TIME

The professor responses to the percentage allocation of their total work time to major duties such as teaching and research. Professors were first asked to state what percentage of their total work time they actually spent on teaching undergraduate or graduate students and what percentage of their total work time they actually spent on research. They were then asked what percentage of their total work time they preferred to devote to teaching and research. It should be noted the percentages allocated to teaching and research across actual or preferred columns does not total 100 because a certain percentage of time could be allocated to other activities such as administration, service, professional growth, or outside consulting. The results show that economics professors say they spend a larger percentage (50) of their actual work time teaching than do most of their peers (44). The differences are slight across most of the Courses. Only professors in the Biological sciences report devoting substantially less actual time in percentage terms to teaching (34). Economics professors would prefer to spend only 41 percent of their time teaching. This preferred time allocation to teaching is the same as for professors in the Social and Physical Sciences. Professors of Business Management, Mathematics and Statistics, and Computer Science want to allocate a little more time to teaching than do economics professors. Only professors in the Biological Sciences show less preference for teaching than professors in all other Courses. The response of economics professors to these actual and preferred questions related to teaching are suggestive.

First, it is at odds with the teaching output of economics professors because they reported teaching slightly fewer classes and fewer students, on average, than most other professors. Second, the differences in actual and preferred time devoted to teaching is greater in economics than in any other Course. Most professors, with the exception of engineers, would prefer to devote less time to teaching compared to what they actually do, but economics professors want more of a change than any other group, perhaps because they think less of teaching or feel more burdened by it.

Economics professors say they spend 30 percent of their total work time on research. This percentage is at the average for other professors, but there are Course differences. Economics professors say they spend more time doing research than professors in Business, Computer Science, the Social sciences, and Engineering. Professors in the physical and Biological sciences report allocating more work time to research, which may be one reason they publish more journal articles. There are also differences in preferred time allocations. Economists would like to spend 43 percent of the time doing research, which is about the same reference as professors in the Physical Sciences. Professors in the Biological sciences desire more time to do research than economists. Business, Engineering, and Social-science professors prefer to spend only about a third of their time on research. There is a certain amount of job dissatisfaction in the area of research because professors in all Courses prefer to allocate more work time to research than they actually do. This result is not surprising given that these professors were trained to do research, and they are located at research universities. The differences among the Courses, however, are striking. The gap in actual to preferred time allocation for research is thirteen percentage points for economics and only Seven percentage points for all other Courses. These results show that economics professors are the least satisfied with their research time even though the actual time they report doing research is quite comparable to most other Courses. This great desire to reallocate time to research may explain the great desire to spend less time teaching.

## IV. REASON FOR LEAVING

Another way to gauge the commitment of economists to teaching and research is to ask a question about what reasons might motivate a professor to change jobs.Table 3 reports the percentage saying "Not Important" (NI) or "Very Important" (VI) to the teaching and research options. The somewhat important category was omitted for the sake of parsimony. The results show

TABLE 2

**Actual and Preferred use of Total Work**

| Sr. No. | Course/field | Teaching | | Research | |
|---|---|---|---|---|---|
| | | Actual | Preferred | Actual | Preferred |
| 1. | Economics | 50 | 41 | 30 | 43 |
| 2. | Other Courses | 44 | 41 | 32 | 39 |
| | (i) Social Science | 46 | 41 | 26 | 34 |
| | (ii) Biological Sciences | 34 | 32 | 46 | 51 |
| | (iii) Physical Sciences | 45 | 41 | 35 | 42 |
| | (iv) Mathematics/Statistics | 49 | 45 | 31 | 39 |
| | (v) Computer Sciences | 49 | 47 | 25 | 30 |
| | (vi) Engineering | 46 | 46 | 26 | 32 |
| | (vii) Business Management | 48 | 44 | 24 | 33 |

that greater opportunity to teach was viewed by economics professors as an inconsequential reason to change a job. Almost seven in 10 economics professors rated it as not important. This response was greater than for any other group of professors. The disparity was greatest (29 to 35 percentage points) when economist's responses are compared with those of professors in Computer Science, Engineering, or Business Management. The rating differences were less, but still substantial (14 to 19 percentage points) when compared with professors in the Social, Biological, or Physical Sciences, or Mathematics and Statistics. The results from this question suggest that economics professors have the least interest in teaching among professors in all science Courses. By contrast, the interest of economics professors in research is substantial and greater than colleagues in other Courses. Almost six in ten economics professors consider greater opportunities to do research to be a very important reason to change jobs. Faculty members in other Courses are also enthusiastic about greater research opportunities as a reason to change jobs, but to a lesser degree depending on the Courses. Only 6 percent of economists say that research opportunities are not important, by far the smallest percentage of any group, whereas large percentages of other groups gave this response.

TABLE 3

**Greater Opportunity to Teach or do Research**

| Sr. No. | Course/field | Teaching | | Research | |
|---|---|---|---|---|---|
| | | Not Important (NI) | Very Important (VI) | Not Important (NI) | Very Important (VI) |
| 1. | Economics | 69 | 8 | 6 | 59 |
| 2. | Other Courses | 47 | 17 | 16 | 51 |
| (i) | Social Science | 50 | 15 | 15 | 49 |
| (ii) | Biological Sciences | 52 | 12 | 11 | 58 |
| (iii) | Physical Sciences | 55 | 9 | 12 | 53 |
| (iv) | Mathematics/Statistics | 51 | 17 | 19 | 49 |
| (v) | Computer Sciences | 34 | 28 | 22 | 50 |
| (vi) | Engineering | 38 | 26 | 18 | 49 |
| (vii) | Business Management | 40 | 22 | 27 | 38 |

## V. PROMOTION, RESEARCH AND TEACHING

A third way to understand the views of economists on the trade-offs between teaching and research is to ask them how these two outputs should be used when making promotion decisions. Faculty members were asked if they agree or disagree with one teaching statement "Teaching effectiveness should be the primary criterion for promotion of faculty/instructional staff at this institution" and one research statement "Research/publications should be the primary criterion for promotion of faculty/ instructional staff at this institution." Response choices were: strongly agree, agree, disagree, and strongly disagree. Economists at research institutions further differentiate themselves from other professors on the issue of teaching as the primary promotion criterion. Less than two in 10 economics professors agreed or strongly agreed that teaching should be the primary criterion for promotion. The support for teaching as the primary promotion criterion rises across the other Courses.

There is agreement from about three in 10 in the physical and Biological sciences or in Mathematics and Statistics, about four in 10 in the other Social sciences, and about five in 10 in Computer Sciences, Engineering, and Business.

On this question economics professors are clearly the outlier group and show the greatest distain for teaching. Of course when the same issue is posed in terms of research as the primary promotion criterion, economics professors are the most enthusiastic of any group. Almost eight in 10 economists agree or strongly agree that research should be the primary promotion criterion, but only about five in 10 of the Business or Computer Science professors responded affirmatively to this item, and only about six in 10 of professors in the other Courses expressed agreement. There are more reservations about using research as the primary promotion criterion among professors in other scientific Courses than there are among professors in economics.

## VI. CONCLUSION

In the education system many economics professors who are working in the universities have a low regard for teaching and high regard for research as part of the employment duties of a professor. The evidence is remarkably consistent whether the question concerns time allocation, job opportunities, or promotion decisions. The consequence of such an attitude is that teaching can be denigrated and undervalued in a profession that has much to offer to the education of undergraduate and graduate students. It may explain why there is so little investment of faculty member time in developing or using alternatives to lecture in undergraduate instruction. Most of the teachers gives limited attention paid to the teaching preparation of undergraduate students.

The results for economics would also not be surprising if the same general conclusion could be drawn for the views of professors in other scientific Courses at research universities. That conclusion, however, does not hold for professors in other Social Sciences, Biological Sciences, Physical Sciences, Mathematics and Statistics, Engineering, Computer Science, and Business. Although there is less support for teaching and more support for research among professors in the Biological and Physical Sciences than in the other Courses included in the study, it is surprising that physical and Biological scientists are not nearly as extreme in their views of the teaching and research tradeoffs as are economics professors.

## References

Allgood, Sam; Bosshardt, 'What Students Remember and Say about College Economics Years Later', *American Economic Review,* 2004.

Becker, William E. 'Teaching Economics to Undergraduates', *Journal of Economic Literature,* September 1997.

Becker, William E. and Watts, Michael. 'Teaching Economics at the Start of the 21st Century: Still Chalk and Talk', *American Economic Review,* 2001.

D.M. Mithani, 'Managerial Economics: Theory and Application', HPH, New Delhi.

M.L. Jhingan, 'Micro Economics', Vrinda Publications, New Age International Publishers Delhi.

Richard G. Lipsey, 'Introduction to Positive Economics', Prentice Hall Publications, New Delhi.

Walstad, William B. 'The Instructional Use and Teaching Preparation of Graduate Students', *American Economic Review,* 2003.

# Education in New Socio-economic Order

S.K.L. DAS AND BISHNU RAY

21st century has brought with it a new socio-economic order in the world. Explosion of information technology has reduced the world into a global village. Distances have become immaterial. Any event irrespective with its importance, it is known to everybody throughout the world. Today the needs of one part of the world can be met by the people of the other part. So the development in one part immediately affects the other part of the globe. Last century saw Quality and Management as important factors for the growth of any community or group. Today situation is changing very fast. Every three months we have something new in a computer. A new computer design can immediately reach to all corners of the world. So unless we are able to make new designs at a very fast rate, we shall be out of market. In the emerging socio-economic scenario it is creativity that will empower a society to take lead in the growth pattern.

Hence, education must respond to this important need of the changing times. The globalisation has led to globalisation of skills. It also demands generation of skills of high order. The situation is gradually becoming so alarming that either we develop creativity or be prepared to perish. It requires rethinking in the whole strategy of teaching and learning economics mainly in undergraduate and postgraduate level. This is not only true of IT sector it is true of all sectors- be it science, engineering or economics.

There is another angle to the whole issue also. There is a change in the global market. Revolution in Information Technology has made it possible to have information available at the door step. Thus, all over the world there is a change in the nature of skills for employment. It is no longer required to mug up facts and reproduce them at an appropriate time. The days of employment on the basis of knowledge in a particular subject are over. Generally today employers do not look for knowledge in a particular subject rather they look for certain skills. A learner of humanities may be engaged in IT sector if she/he has developed skills of analysis, thinking, etc. If we analyze the pattern of interview/tests for recruitment in major employment sectors such as IT, media sector, social sector, etc. we find that they do not go for knowledge in a subject rather they look for skills of various kinds. This necessitates the urgency to look for changes in the strategy of teaching learning process.

## Core Creative Competencies

Now the question arises as to which type of skills we should develop. On the basis of scientific analysis of the flow of information in brain it has been found at APCL that the following Core Creative Competencies (C3) are the basic competencies which one is required to develop in the course of any learning programme. In fact, it is these competencies which are tested by the recruitment agencies these days.

- Concentration
- Memory
- Thinking
- Power of Observation
- Imagination
- Emotional Management
- Power of Expression

A learning programme should be so designed that it

develops these core creative competencies. Facts should be so placed and used that they are helpful in the development of skills. That is why subject based learning are becoming irrelevant and multidisciplinary approach is becoming the order of the day.

**Adopt Skill-based Approach to Learning**

Any subject basically comprises of a set of information and skills. Our teaching process emphasizes more on getting the information rather than acquisition of those skills. In economics we are more concerned about learning what the facts and figures of the society are. But we are not so much concerned about developing the skills such as collection of facts, appreciation of evolution/change of an activity over a period of time, their analysis, deducing inference, etc. which economics teaching is expected to impart. There is so much emphasis on ideas of different economists that development of skills, related to processing of information, is neglected. In changing times there is a strong case for changing subject based approach to skill-based approach.

The real question is how to do it. It is suggested that present information-based approach must give way to constructive approach. It implies that learners must be given opportunity to learn by construction. This has been traditionally known as learning by doing. In the present context economics teaching should not limit itself to books written by eminent economists/ econometricians, but it should empower a learner to have an independent evaluation of the facts and come to their own conclusion. Today learners must become apt in making their own hypothesis; they should know how to test them and to come to final conclusion.

Here history of science teaching can be of great help to us. The growth of science made rapid strides when laboratory approach was adopted. Laboratory approach is complementary and supplementary to classroom teaching. Facts can be taught in the class and skills should be developed in laboratories. Here power of observation can be developed by collection of information, hypothesis can be made and tested and independent decisions can be taken.

Laboratory activities are helpful in better understanding. They help in putting abstract ideas into practice. They also help in taking learning closer to life and thus help in bringing contextual relevance to education. They lead to development of scientific temper and attitude, which is the base of democratic orientation. Classrooms cater mainly to verbal and logical intelligence. Laboratories can be designed to cover activities of all intelligence. This way they help in ensuring success to all in the learning process. Laboratories provide opportunity for experimentation and thus help in development of creativity.

It is said: We learn

- 10% of what we read
- 20% of what we hear
- 30% of what we see
- 50% of what we both see and hear
- 70% of what we discuss with others
- 80% of what we experience personally (emotional)
- 95% of what we teach others

Classroom teaching is static whereas labs provide dynamism to learning. Lab provides an opportunity for holistic learning. One is able to test one's ideas and come to independent conclusion. Hence, lab approach of learning leads to development of skills of independent thinking and judgement. In a subject like economics where one is required to assess facts and come to judgement, lab approach can be the better way of learning.

It is to be noted that this laboratory may not be a store house of equipments as science laboratory. In fact, they are just a place to facilitate performance of activity.

## EXPERIMENTAL ECONOMICS

Standard assumptions of economics Consistent with its role in studying economic behaviour, the types of experiments that would be performed in the lab fall into three broad categories: (1) studies of individual decision-making behaviour; (2) studies of strategic behaviour in groups (i.e. tests of equilibrium); and (3) studies of how the design of institutions and markets affects welfare.

Specifically, in studying individual decisions, our primary interest will are, or are not, followed by experimental subjects, what systematic variations there are from those assumptions, and what impact this has on individual choices. In studying strategic behaviour, our main interest is in finding classes of situations in which standard economic concepts of equilibrium succeed (or systematically fail) in predicting strategic behaviour in games or markets. Finally, we see our lab as providing a test bed for the design of legislative, economic, and social institutions (e.g., effective deregulated energy markets) with particular care given to the intersection of psychology and economics in the design of these institutions. The users of the laboratory will come from almost all areas of the social sciences, especially those interested in individual choice and economic outcomes. Investigators will be drawn from diverse units like different educational institutions including the technical institutions, management schools, industrial units, financial markets, members of policy-makers the Department of Agricultural and Resource Economics, the College of Letters and Sciences, the School of Information Management and Systems, and the College of Engineering. Within the School of Business, it will include researchers from the areas of finance, marketing, economics, and organisational behaviour. In Arts and Letters, users will come from areas as diverse as economics, political science, psychology and sociology. Fundamentals of Individual Behaviour, Psychologists and economists are currently exploring together a wide variety of ways in which individual behaviour deviates from the standard utility maximisation traditionally assumed of economic agents. These endeavors take two forms. First, economic agents may have one function that expresses their true welfare, yet they may maximize another. Psychologists have developed remarkably clever tests to demonstrate such seemingly contradictory behaviour. An alternative hypothesis is that economic agents are maximizing correctly, but that conventional economic assumptions about just what matters to them are incorrect or incomplete. Empirical work with standard utility theory as the benchmark has established a whole array of deviating behaviours. It has long been shown that individual decision-making depends upon how a situation is framed. Indeed, the classic social psychology findings of Milgram, Asch and Tajfel, that individual decision-making is remarkably determined by perceptions of the context, has been demonstrated over the gamut of almost all social psychology and economic experiments. These results should not come as a surprise; they reflect the dictum from sociology that behaviour depends upon the "definition of the situation." But by bringing scientific precision to this dictum, the economic and psychological laboratory has shown how this wisdom from sociology in fact applies to a wide variety of decision-making and expands greatly behaviour, beyond the traditional model of economic man. Matthew Rabin of Berkeley has been prominent in translating these findings into revisions of standard economic models. In sum, then the wide range of deviations from maximisation of utility with only classic economic arguments in the utility function is the subject of laboratory experimentation. This exploration, which has been central to the development of behavioural economics, necessitates the use of laboratory facilities.

The mission of the Social Entrepreneur Center is to promote the use of technology for social issues by creating sustainable economic experiments.

**Break the Barriers of Subjects**

One of the major requirements of the modern teaching is that it breaks the barriers of subjects. Today Economists should know the basics of mathematics, psychology, sociology and Political conditions, physical and cultural conditions of the society. In fact, economics is related to all walks of life and thus there is a need to introduce analytical tools of science and mathematics to make economics learning more objective. For this purpose experts from Science and Mathematics may be associated with teaching of economics. One may even think of a basic course of Science and Mathematics for the students of economics. Similarly, we should have a basic computer course for all learners. As a first step we should start a laboratory for research purposes and later it should be incorporated in our teaching process.

Similarly, there is also a need to study history of different subjects. A learner of mathematics should know the history of mathematics or a learner of science should know the history of science.

**Applying Knowledge to Daily Life**

A learner is often amazed as to why he learns economics. Is it only to learn the concept of classical to modern economists?

Is it collection of economic data that happened in the past? Where will he apply the knowledge? It is said 'where there are six economists, there are seven opinions.' But where do we provide opportunity to them to apply the basic concept of economics in day to day life and to predict future course of actions. One of the major concerns is to prepare our children in the science of applying knowledge of applied economics for finding the solutions of maximisation of utility with the help of scarce means which everybody is facing in daily life.

**Nature of Equipments and Materials in Economic Lab**

It is difficult to list out the nature of materials and equipments in experimental economic lab, as it would depend on the status of technology in the area. A very good lab may even have facility of chemical analysis or even carbon dating. It may also have scanning facility. However, some of the simple items may be listed as follows:

- Audio Visual Cassettes
- Cassette Recorder
- Computers
- Facility for the editing of multimedia presentation
- Multimedia CDs
- Cards
- Materials from past economic activities
- Materials from market analysis
- Microscope
- Scale
- Weighing Machine
- Survey Equipments
- Camera
- Interview sheets
- Facility for modeling
- Old papers and magazines

**Nature of Activities**

In the laboratory following types of activities may be performed.

- Projects
- Games
- Interview
- Survey
- Observation activities

Visit to agro-based rural areas, industrial areas, market complex and developmental projects going on different places. Social auditing of different government projects for eliminating unemployment and poverty.

Case study of different projects and class room experiments, etc.

**Themes for Activities in the Lab**

Another question is to how to select theme for activities in the lab. One principle of selecting themes in creative learning process is to move from known to unknown. Thus themes should be so selected that initially we should start learning process from individual him/herself. Then one should take up themes related to family matters. Thereafter, one should expand to neighbourhood. Neighbourhood consists of friends, institutions, village, town, natural objects, local heroes, etc. The area of neighbourhood should gradually go on increasing.

In the context of economics one should start with the economic history of family, village and towns and gradually go to state, country and other areas of world. This is contrary to the existing practice where local economic condition is completely ignored. Hence, one is not able to apply one's knowledge to practice. Understanding about local economic situation may be useful in developing self-confidence and social awareness which is a primary requirement for any creative learning process. We should also choose themes to take care of local eco-cultural needs.

**Examples of Activities in Classroom Experiment in Economics**

Classroom experiments are effective because students are placed directly into the economic environments being studied. One of the most exciting recent developments in the teaching of economics is the increased use of classroom exercises that insert students directly into the economic environments being studied. For example, students who participate in market trading as buyers and sellers come away impressed with the strong pressures to trade at a uniform price. This reaction is then mixed with surprise when they later discover that the observed price standard is the competitive price determined by the intersection of supply and demand functions constructed from information that was not available to any single trader. Even when standard theories fail, they can fail in interesting ways, e.g. when trading prices for assets veer away from present value fundamentals during price bubbles (Ball and Holt, 1998). Regardless of the outcomes of classroom experiments, the structural parameters of standard theories are determined by individual incentives and the rules specified in the instructions, so theoretical predictions can be calculated and used as a benchmark of comparison. As economics has become more technical, even at the undergraduate level, the use of classroom experiments provides an important connection between theories and key features of the markets and institutions being studied. Before surveying specific applications, it will be useful to discuss the origins and role of classroom experiments, as well as some general advice about procedures and pitfalls.

Traditionally, economics has not been an experimental science, and this fact has shaped the kinds of questions addressed and arguments presented. Keynes (1936) stressed the important role of conversation and criticism in evaluating economic arguments, "...where it is often impossible to bring one's ideas to a conclusive test either formal or experimental." As a result, theories often rose or fell in popularity on the basis of generality, mathematical elegance, or clever terminology. Samuelson (1947) noted that economics lacked the "self-cleansing" nature of a hard science, and therefore he stressed the methodology of deriving comparative static predictions of changes of observable variables. Ironically, at about the same time, Chamberlin (1948) was conducting the first in-class market experiments, which began a process of changing what we think of as being observable. Chamberlin had his students (doctoral students at Harvard) circulate around the room and bargain. Some were sellers, with numbered cards that determined their costs, and others were buyers, with numbered cards that determined their redemption values. Once a price was negotiated, the seller would earn the difference between the price and the cost, and the buyer would earn the difference between the redemption (or "resale") value and the price. The use of cards (e.g. playing cards) to distribute confidential information to subjects is a common feature of many of the classroom experiments.

Laboratory experiments have had a particularly strong influence on the development of game theory. Two of the three recipients of the first Nobel Prize that recognized game theory, Reinhard Selten and John Nash, used laboratory experiments early on in their work. Nash apparently participated first as a subject in someone else's experiment at RAND, and his sister recalls him earning $50 a day in 1952 "to play games." Nash was a coauthor on one bargaining experiment, but the unexpected results discouraged him from continuing, as he veered back into the world of pure mathematics, and other afflictions. In contrast, Selten remains an active experimentalist and has become increasingly interested learning and models of bounded rational behaviour as ways of explaining observed laboratory results.

Many classroom experiments today involve simple games, even if they are dressed up in the context of some substantive application to law and economics, industrial organisation, public choice, etc.

The work of Smith, Selten, and others later stimulated an ever-expanding amount of research experiments, which are surveyed in Davis and Holt (1993), and Kagel and Roth (1995).

Playing cards are used to induce supply and demand functions. Instructions and helpful hints are provided. The exercise facilitates an understanding and appreciation of the robustness and efficiency of the textbook model of perfect competition. The supply and demand model is the centerpiece of any introductory microeconomics course. An effective way to introduce this model is to put students into a situation that resembles trading on the floor or "pit" of some commodities futures markets. After the negotiated prices have stabilised, the participants can be shown market parameters and asked to explain why the prices converged to the observed levels. The objective is to have students discover the supply and demand model, and to realize that "large number" of traders are not necessary for obtaining efficient, competitive outcomes. The classroom market can also be used to illustrate a variety of other factors: the effects of price controls, shifts in demand or supply, and more. Playing cards can be used to distribute value and cost information quickly and confidentially to the students. With 10-25 participants, it takes from 40 minutes to an hour read the instructions and go through several 5-minute trading periods. Begin by dividing the class into equal numbers of buyers and sellers, leaving two or three people out to be assistants. Each buyer is given a "red" card (hearts or diamonds), and each seller is given a "black" card (clubs or spades). Buyers can earn money by purchasing at prices below the "value" numbers on their cards, and the sellers can earn money by selling at prices above the "cost" numbers on their cards. For example, if a buyer with a red 10 and a seller with a black 2 agree on a price of Rs. 5, then the buyer earns Rs. 5 and the seller earns Rs. 3. Sellers are not permitted to sell below cost, and buyers are not permitted to pay more than the value of a unit. Thus each buyer has a perfectly inelastic demand for one unit at any price below the buyer's card number, and each seller has a perfectly inelastic supply at any price above the seller's card number. All buyers and sellers receive a single card at the beginning of a trading period. The resulting market demand and supply curves will be step functions, as shown on the left side of figure 1. The cards used for the for the solid line D and S curves in this figure are: Black (spades or clubs): 2, 2, 3, 4, 5, 6, 6, 7, 8

**Red (hearts or diamonds): 10, 10, 9, 8, 7, 6, 6, 5, 4**

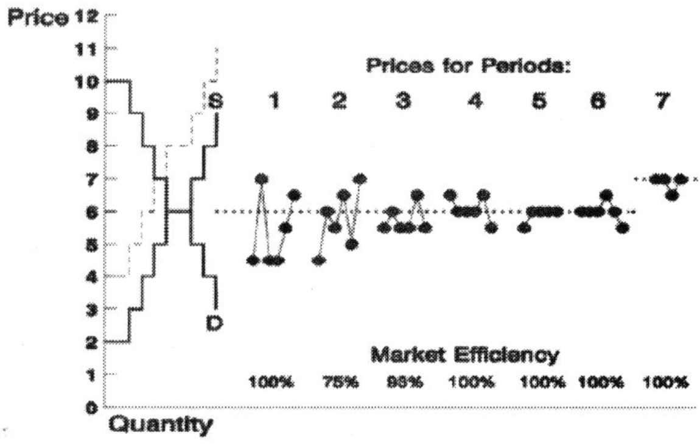

The competitive price of 6, which is obvious from the graph, will not be at all obvious to the traders who have only their own value or cost information. The equilibrium quantity prediction in this example is a range from 5 to 7 units.

After the cards are distributed, the participants are called to a trading area in the front of the room to begin negotiations. When a buyer and a seller agree on a price, they proceed to the recording desk, where the price is checked, announced, and written on the blackboard. The right supply and demand model is the centerpiece of any introductory microeconomics course. An effective way to introduce this model is to put students into a situation that resembles trading on the floor or "pit" of some commodities futures markets. After the negotiated prices have stabilised, the participants can be shown market parameters and asked to explain why the prices converged to the observed levels. The objective is to have students discover the supply and demand model themselves, and to realize that "large numbers" of traders are not necessary for obtaining efficient, competitive outcomes. The classroom market can also be used to illustrate a variety of other factors: the effects of price controls, shifts in demand or supply, and more. Playing cards can be used to distribute value and cost information quickly and confidentially to the students.

The standard macroeconomic models used in undergraduate courses are presented at a high level of aggregation that is a common source of complaint. The upshot of this is that intermediate microeconomics courses are often unpopular with students as well as faculty. With the help of classroom experiments, as done by Jacob K. Georee and Charles A. Holt of USA in their paper, the course structure can be more beneficial to the students of economics and it can be made more popular and practical. Similarly money creation by classroom games can also be experimented, as done by Susan K. Lucy of University of South Carolina. In the classroom laboratory students are engaged in the process of money creation, via a circle of loans and deposits. With this process students can have a complete practical knowledge of monetary policy, experimental economics and other areas of economic science. The basic objective is to demonstrate how an initial injection of resources leads to a multiple increase in deposits. Technique of experimental economics to set-up a classroom situation where students have clear ideas of Statistical problems like Bayes' rule, which has always been a useful tool in the analysis of economic data. Bayes' rule provides a natural bridge between simple intuition and the mathematical formula. This rule is included in the syllabus of undergraduate courses in economic statistics, game theory and managerial economics. Recently its importance in economic theory has increased as result of the study of markets with asymmetric information or with uncertainty about distributions of wages, prices and others fields of economic analysis. The teaching of Bayes' rule can be made more realistic with classroom experiment, as done by Charles A. Holt and Lisa Anderson of University of Virginia (USA).

## SUGGESTIONS

No doubt keeping in view of changing economic conditions, different universities have thoroughly revised its syllabus in economics and other subjects, but Universities of Bihar and Jharkhand adopted the syllabus, which is more or less in the old pattern. The basic considerations of the goals and objectives are to create value orientation and employment opportunities for the students. The academic and research programmes are designed to fulfil the needs of the trade, industry and society. The needs of the growing economy and market are incorporated in our academic programmes. The curriculum development committee comprising of subject experts from industry and academicians along with Alumni should meet every year to finalize the syllabus of economics.

Course structure in undergraduate and postgraduate level should be so designed which will suit the changing conditions. It should be essential for the students to have at least 8 weeks training in undergraduate level and 8 weeks summer training along with one minor research work for postgraduate students. For skilled development of our young students, Developmental workshops, Annual programmes, Seminars should be made compulsory in the Department, for which financial and infrastructures should be provided to the department. Besides class room interactions, a case study analysis and for practical exposures for each student through campus industry interactions should be incorporated into the syllabus. Case studies should be made compulsory elements of all programmes. Economics Department should introduce new syllabus in which students have to make presentations and assignments. Personality development workshops should be regular features.

Recently our students have been entrusted to make a social audit of NAREGA in Tundi Block of Dhanbad. They have done it very successfully. They were involved to find out the BPL family in their areas and to file a report to the District administration. Our students have done it in a proper manner. I think such type of case study should be incorporated in Postgraduate level to enhance practical knowledge among the students.

For skilled development "Economic Laboratory" should be established in each college, which will certainly change the entire learning process. Creativity is more important than theoretical knowledge. Higher education in Economics is not merely a tool for finding suitable employment; but it is the breeding ground for ideas critical of and critical to the development of the nation as well as the society. Hence creative learning is more important. I have made a case study of the students of a school at Patna, "A School of Creative Learning" and found that students were involved in different activities from standard I to standard X and they had gained more practical knowledge. Learning economics creatively can be of great help in the era of globalisation and it is possible when technique of experimental economics will be set-up in classroom situation where students learn to make micro and macro economic analysis.

Hence my submission is to recast the present syllabus which can develop the Core Creative Competencies among the students of economics in undergraduate and postgraduate level. Creative Learning in Economics can certainly develop the skill in students and teachers both, which is the need of the hour.

## References

Douglas and Charles A. Holt (1993), Experimental Economics, Princeton University Press.

Goeree, Jacob K. (1999), Employment and Prices in a Simple Micro-economy, *Southern Economic Journal*, 65(3): 637-47.

Goeree, Jacob K. and Charles A. Holt (2000), Employment and prices in the simple Macroeconomy.

Grether, David M., Testing Bayes' Rule: Some Experimental Evidence, *Journal of Economic Behaviour and Organisation* (1992).

Holt, Charles A. 1996, Trading in Pit Market, *Journal of Economic Persepective* 10(i): 193-205.

Samuelson Paul A., Foundation of Economic Analysis.

Syllabus of D.U./UGC and other Indian Universities.

UGC Guidelines SAP.

# Teaching in Economics at Undergraduate Level in Rural (Mufassil) Colleges

## A Great Challenge (A Case Study of Jharkhand)

N.C. JHA AND AWADESH KUMAR SINHA

Since independence, there is undoubtedly all round development of education in India because it is one of important keys of sustainable development of any country especially the developing one which involves a process of learning through which a human being passes from infancy to maturity as in Sanskrit it is observed as 'TAMSOMA JYOTIR GAMAYA'. This aptly describes the purpose of the education—To lead from darkness (ignorance) to light (knowledge). During the 62 years of educational development, it is found that it is indeed phenomenonal but still the literacy rate is not at par with the developed nations. The system of education in India is divided into five broad levels—Primary, Secondary, Intermediate, Graduate and Postgraduate. The higher education begins with intermediate having three faculties—Arts, Science and Commerce-some professional courses. After doing this, the students move forward to graduation-level—general-bachelor in Arts, Science,

Commerce (with honours or General one), Technical Education, Engineering, Medical, Agriculture, Professional Education—B.B.A., B.T.M, B.C.A., and so many branches. After doing this, they also move towards postgraduate level in different discipline—faculties with different subjects. It is found that the number of universities as well as colleges is rising at a rapid rate both in government managed and private managed. In Technical, Professional courses, the private participation is rising at leaps and bound.

In India, University Grant Commission (U.G.C.) which was established in 1956 has been given the responsibility to take urgent steps to increase for promotion and co-ordination of university education. It has also been made responsible for determination and maintenance of standards in teaching, examination and research in university to fulfil its objectives. The role of the state in higher education has been recognized, as the Radhakrishna Commission observes, the state should recognize its responsibility for financing of higher education. In recent years, whatever is the planned budget, the allocation towards the higher education is found a diminishing trend although in principle, 6% of G.D.P. is being said to be provided for the education. But the proportion for higher education is found at worse because over the years/plans, the percentage expenditure to G.D.P. is declining.

Jharkhand which is one of the new states comes into existence on 15$^{th}$ of Nov., 2000, better known as the tribal state of Indian union, having geographical area 79.7 thousand sq.km. and 26.9 million population; out of which 27.67% tribal population predominantly rural in character where 64.9% population lives below the poverty line against the national average 25% (in 2006-07) but the main cause of concern for the poverty which is the result is the illiteracy because in literacy Map of India, this state ranks 34$^{th}$ of 35$^{th}$ states and union territories, having the literacy rate 54.13% against the national average 65%. There is wide disparity in rate of literacy among the regions of Jharkhand which varies been 29.03% (for Palamue, Rural) to 71.13% (Santhal Parganas Urban). The state of higher education in this state is also a great concern because of poverty and illiteracy, the parents fail to send their children towards college/postgraduate level

In the present era, undoubtedly Economics is dominating the world stage like never before. No person can be considered educated without a sound knowledge of certain basics of this subject. Whether it is lower level of course examination/ competitive examination or the higher level of examination or interviews more and more questions are focused on economic issues even in G.D. Interviews, too the questions are based on economics for which teaching in economics is now a day an important act because in the state of literate world, the awareness programme associated with price rise,poverty, illiteracy, development and other variables have already been understood either by literacy materials or experience process.

In class teaching, this subject is equally important subject in all three streams—Arts, Science and Commerce at the Intermediate level. This subject is opted more by the Science students because of C.B.S.E.-based syllabus in which except one core literature subject, every student has to read four Subjects- two compulsory—Physics and chemistry and two optional—Mathematics, Biology, Economics, Computer, Science, etc. Hence Science students generally opt economics as one of optional subjects because the burden of both Mathematics and Biology could not be borne. In case of Commerce faculties, it is a compulsory subject. But for Arts students this Subject is an optional one and majority of students in this faculty fear to opt economics because of some mathematical and analytical concept associated in the courses of study. In general, the Arts students are weak in Mathematics and do not adopt such difficult subjects. Although a few students who are laborious and have better family background essentially opt this subject because the parents induce them, who know that in higher education in any professional courses, it is being taught and very significant one.

In rural or mufassil colleges, where the students go for higher education have not so many goals rather than to obtain a certificate or degree so that something could be done for earning the subsistence income such as the work at shop or writing the documents of pleaders/doctors/businessmen/or to practice the home private tuition that's why they are not much interested towards the subjects especially this subject; secondly, in rural colleges, it is found that students have a practice to attend seasonal classes or even never attend the classes because of some more important home related works. They prefer to work at field to attend the class because the parents of rural areas also compel them. This is because of massive poverty and illiteracy on the parts of parents. The classes in such rural/semi-urban-based colleges are not held regularly because of very thin attendance or disinterest of students on the one hand the less number of teacher as well as lack of proper and sufficient infra-structure. In Jharkhand, many a college especially in rural/semi-urban-based there is either two or even only one teacher in Economics department. In case of Madhupur college, Madhupur, which is a constituent unit of SIDO-KANHU-MURMU UNIVERSITY, DUMKA, there is only one teacher in this subject where as there are about 1800 students in Intermediate level and about 150 students at degree level. Do you think that how can a single teacher teach economics with high quality efficiency in classes?

To the teacher concerned, teaching in economics in undoubtedly very interesting but the teacher has to face a heavy work load—five to six lectures per day, i.e. 42 or 35 or on average 35 classes in a week. The students presence in classes are sometime very very thin. When the teacher is in leave for some reasons, the classes are declared as suspended. Due to irregular holding of university examination of degree-level, the classes are also declared as suspended because of less number of teaching staff and very limited infrastructure. Moreover, the availability of higher institutions—college with Graduate level teaching is very limited and the JAC is increasing only the number of seats for admission without creating the number of teaching and Non-teaching posts. This has created many problems in the college premises and the teaching is the worst affected.

### Qualification for Admission in Graduate Level Economic (Honours) General

A student may be admitted in graduate studies-degree/bachelor of Arts Economics (Hons or General), he/she must have passed +2 level/Intermediate-level examination from board/university—having one of the subjects as Economics; provided that for admission to the course of instruction for honours degree in economics, it shall be necessary for a student to have obtained not less than 45% marks. On the other hand, for subsidiary/general course, the subject can be opted by those students who have simply passed +2 Intermediate-level with economics as one of the subjects.

## Minimum Requirement of Instruction

No fewer than five lecturers in a week shall be delivered in each paper—at least the number of tutorials in an Honours subject not be less than two—at least one period of tutorial instructions for subsidiary/general one. Any registered-student of this subject of the university who is admitted in B.A. (General/ Hons) D-1, D-2 and D-3 examination if he produces a certificate from the principal of a college of—

(a) good conduct,
(b) completion of regular courses of study in the college by fulfilment of the prescribed requirement of attendance of lectures tutorials and by satisfactory record tutorials, and
(c) having passed the college test or any other equivalent examination for making him eligible for university examination.

## Courses of Study Offered by the University of Jharkhand

In earlier days, the course study in economics—in Honours as well as in general vary from one university to another with some basic similarities of teaching Economic theory, Money, Banking and International trade, Keynesian Economics, Indian Economy, Public Finance, Economic growth and development, statistics, and with certain specialised subjects/Papers. But from 2002-03 on wards, when U.G.C. courses of study for three year degree course—Part-I, Part-II, Part-III introduced all the universities of India for Universalication of Single Syllabus, there is no window of discripencies. At present in graduation level for economic honours course, the students will have to study two papers—Microeconomics and Macroeconomics respectively for Honours, for general/subsidiary one paper-consisting of Micro, Macro public finance and International trade, In Degree Part-II, there are two papers for Honours course—III Paper—Indian Economy—IV Paper—Group A—Public Finance Group B—History of Economic thought, for general/Subsidiary Course-II Papers—Indian Economy. The courses of study for degree Part-III have been enlarged since there are four papers for Honours Students—V Paper—Consisting Eco. Development and Environmental Economics, VI paper—Quantitative Techniques

(Mathematics and Statistics portion) VII Paper—optional one-consisting—Mathematical Economics, Industrial Economics, Industrial Economics, Demography, Banking and Financial Markets—VIII paper—(optional)-consisting—Econometric Method, Economics of Social Sector and Environmental issues, Agricultural Economics, Computer and its Application and for general course student in D-III—Economic Growth, Planning and Environmental Economics are being prescribe the module in those papers in all the university in India remain almost the same.

At Graduation-level the courses of study incorporated with very interesting papers as well as modules. But in this courses of study, some important papers have been ignored such as The economic story of six great nations—G.B., U.S.A., U.S.S.R., Japan and France along with economic history of India. This neglect is not appreciated by the teaching community because the present-era-students cannot know the rise of these economic giants of the world, the Depression of 1929-30, its impact on the world economy including on the Indian economy, other economic historical events occurred in different economies which are indeed essential to be taught to the students because history repeats itself and with historical background many a great knowledge could be anticipated. Moreover, in this course of study in degree Part-III—Quantitative technique is undoubtedly very interesting in teaching but in rural colleges, adds an extra pressure to the student of economics honours because they are not mathematically strong, so opted the Arts stream. This compels the students to opt other subject and make this spreads the ray of fear. If we compare the number of students opted economics as honours with other subjects. Such as History, Political Science and Sociology or other Social Science, we find that there is a great divergence between economics and other subjects. This Mathematical-based paper compels the students not opting Economics as the subject.

## Student-Teacher Ratio

In teaching and learning process, whether in schools or in the institutions of higher education the teacher forms the major input. The number of students per teacher largely determined the effectiveness of contact between the teacher and students.

Therefore students-teacher ratio is considered as an indicator of the effectiveness of student-teacher inertaction. It is seen that if student-teacher ratio is higher, the effectiveness of interaction is poor and therefore the quality of education would be poor. If this ratio is small, the interaction is good and the quality of teaching and learning would also be good.

In the university Departments/colleges of Jharkhand, it is found in general that the student-teacher ratio is very high because the number of teaching post was not created anything more since 1980. At that time the number of students are less. But day-by-day, the number has been rising at an increasing rate especially in +2/intermediate level and graduation level. Thus, it has created a great problem in making student-teacher ratio at an optimum level,that is every twenty students there should be one teacher or 20:1 ratio. But in college at +2 intermediate level it is almost 250:1 or even more especially where there is only one teacher, the ratio is almost abnormal. Let us take the example of Economics Department of Madhupur College, Madhupur, a constituent unit of S.K.M. University, Dumka, where the total students in economics are about 2500 (1924 at intermediate level and rest at graduation level), but out of two sanctioned post, there is only one teacher since one of the teacher has already retired this years and so the student-teacher ratio is 2500: 1. Can you imagine such a ratio and how can a quality education, lectures, be expected? In many colleges of Jharkhand, there is same problems and the teacher remains puzzled how to teach such a large pupils because he has his own limitations, even if he regularly takes five or six general classes, it does not find optimal as prescribed in the courses of study.

**Contact Hours**

The indicatator of student teacher ratio as effectiveness of teaching/learning process is based on the assumption of a certain number of contact hours between students and the teachers. If a teacher does not meet his classes whatever may be the student teacher ratio, effectiveness would be nil. It is, therefore, important to know whether the number of contact hours/lectures periods as planned are taken or not? If not, what is the gap? This gap would determine the degree of effectiveness. The smaller the gap, the greater the effectiveness and *vice-versa*. Therefore, student- teacher ratio analysis is further extended by examining the number of lectures/contact hours as planned and as actually taken.

One might argue that a teacher may go to class may not teach, but that is a rare phenomenon. Even if it is a general one it falls beyond the quantitative economic analysis.

## Plan of Contact Hours

As per new U.G.C. courses of study these are the planned contact hours for the honours subject, subsidiary and general one which we may explain as follows—

**IN HONOURS COURSE**

| CLASS | |
|---|---|
| D-I | —2 CLASSES DAILY × 6 = 12 CLASSES IN A WEEK |
| D-II | —2 CLASSES DAILY × 6 = 12 CLASSES IN A WEEK |
| D-III | —3 CLASSES DAILY × 6 = 18 CLASSES IN A WEEK |

**SUBSIDIARY/GENERAL**

| | |
|---|---|
| D-I | 5 CLASSES IN A WEEK |
| D-II | 5 CLASSES IN A WEEK |
| D-III | 5 CLASSES IN A WEEK |
| TOTAL | 57 CLASSES IN A WEEK |

Hence, in Economics department minimum 57 classes at the graduation level according to the new U.G.C Syllabus should be planned excluding the tutorial classes. The above class contact hours has been planned without taking the holidays on account. If the U.G.C. recommendations of 180 working days are considered, per teacher per week lecture load would be only 4 to 5 lectures per week consider this point also per teachers per week actual number of Lectures/Contact periods taken is not even 1/3$^{rd}$ of the norms of 18 Lectures per week per teacher.

Let us take the example of Economics Department of Madhupur College, Madhupur, a constituent unit of S.K.M. University, Dumka, Jharkhand where there are two sectioned post but one of the teacher is retired on 01/01/2009. The planned contact/Lecture hours are as follows:

| *Class* | *No. of Classes Allotted* |
|---|---|
| I.A. 1ST YEAR | 3 |
| I.A. 2nd YEAR | 3 |
| B.A. (HONS) | |
| D-I | 5 |
| D-II | 5 |
| D-III | 10 |
| B.A GENERAL/SUB— | |
| D-I | 03 |
| D-II | 03 |
| D-III | 03 |
| TOTAL | 35 |

This is quite very high work load to the concerned teacher against the U.G.C. norms and in Jharkhand, most of colleges which are established in semi-urban/rural area even many an urban area college area suffering from this problem and that's why the output at the graduation-level seems very unsatisfactory.

## PERFORMANCE

The performance of students both in honours and pass courses at the graduation level as compared to the higher secondary level is found the poor or very unsatisfactory. If we compare the students of honours course with Subsidiary/General at D-I, and D-II level, the performance of subsidiary/general students is relatively poorer. At the +2 Intermediate level, the proportion of students with higher level of performance is satisfactory but the proportion of students grade rating with higher level of performance (60% and above) is very small, in the university three to five on average, at college, for example, Madhupur College, Madhupur one to two every year—in the final result. Moreover, in three year course of study, the failed/dropped out percentage has a rising trend in economics because out of 40 to 45 students in D-1 honours course, only 8 to 10 students clears the honours course—D-III final with 1 or 2 first class. In case of Subsidiary, the failed/dropped out students are higher than the general course study. Thus the possibility of wastage was greater among the students with poorer performance at the graduation level.

## FINDINGS AND SUGGESTIONS

The above analysis explains the teaching of economics at the graduation level with regard to enrolment, courses of study, quality of students, effectiveness of teaching process viewed from student-teacher ratio and per teacher lecture/contact period per week work load of teacher as determined by U.G.C. and the actual work-load at semi/rural colleges of Jharkhand and the performance of the students as the result. The new U.G.C. courses of study in economics is undoubtedly an improved one but the addition of quantitative method as one of the papers in honours course has created ray of panics on the mind of students of Arts faculty because in general, it is common understanding that in Arts, there is no quantitative teaching paper/mathematical-oriented paper. This paper especially in semi urban/rural area, creates an extra thinking to the students of economics whether to opt economics honours or not and the last result is in less number of honours students because the students are not mathematically sound even at the basic level. That's why more students prefer History Political Science, Sociology, etc. rather than economics even if he/she has opted economics as one of the subject at +2/ Intermediate level.

The quality of students in economics honours is found certainly better than the other honours course in faculty. But because of very high student-teacher ratio in the semi-urban/rural colleges and only clearing course attitude of the students make it difficult and there is a higher failed/dropped out student at the final year results. The work load is very high at the Semi-urban college. The contact hours of the students is very limited which makes a question mark on the effectiveness of the teaching-learning process in the colleges/university of Jharkhand.

## POLICY SUGGESTIONS

It is found that teaching in economics is indeed an interesting act at class-room as well as other places. It reveals us with the theory that teaching in economics and economic development agenda, planning, constraints, etc. are inseparably linked in a kind seed and flower relationship. But there is serious constraint or limiting factor in teaching in economics because the failure rate at the graduation level especially in Honours course is above 60% or more for which a number of factors are responsible, the inescapable conclusion is that result in this subject is better in those areas and colleges where there are good qualified devoted teachers and they are mostly in urban areas, where the students also understand the subject importance rather than opting the other relatively easy subjects. At this level also admission by and large, should be regulated in such a way that only the better motivated students gain entry into this subject especially at honours level. But the present enrolment policy is also responsible for low percentage result because if a student any how gets 45% in this subject gets the honours course admission even if he has no interest. Thus the university as well as college administration should close the 'open door admission policy' in this subject.

For better result and better conceptually trained pupils the university as well as colleges should develop better Infra-structure, Library, computer application and trained devoted economics teachers because a good teacher can certainly change the whole face of result of this subject. A good devoted teacher should have 'AIR' qualification where A for Accounting, I for Integrity, and R for Responsibility, these three mantras should become our own subject mantras if economics is to survive at all. They are as essential and indispensible mantra for the economics teacher as the air every living being breathes' particularly parents, teachers and parents should assimilate, absorb and enchance the quality of all our teaching in economics at the college or university level. As teacher, we are accountable to our students, to parents who have enthusiastically entrusted their children to their care during the most sensitive and crucial years. Integrity should have the essentiality among the teaching follows because Integrity leading to credibility and reliability and trust is the most essential quality for lasting success and achievement. Moreover teacher of economics should understand the importance of responsibility of those students who opted economics on the belief that he would certainly take care of him. The teacher has no right to neglect those students who have treat him as the leader of future life and helpful in critical position. The teacher should present himself as the role model for the students.

This subject at honours level should be taught by dividing into two parts—Economics (in General form) and Advanced Economics (in Mathematical form). This would give the options among the students because those students who are weak and not interested in Mathematical aptitudes opt general economics, those who are interested in Mathematics, or strong in Mathematical application opt the advanced economics. This would certainly increase the number of students in the department.

Moreover, in the courses of study, the chapter related with business management or business organisation (B.O.), the economic history paper, environmental economics, Forensic economics, Managerial economics should be incorporated. This would certainly helpful in gaining employment opportunities or in taking the admission in professional courses at the highest level.

The performance of a student is measured through the obtaining percentage of marks. There should be a radical change in examination system because the method does not guarantee the real assessment of the students. The Semester system of examination should be practised. Moreover, besides the book-knowledge, the students especially in honours paper should be given for presenting project report/on social dissertation paper environmental, health demography, family economic problems of the Indian economy. This would certainly develop the creative and analytical skill among the students of economics.

Moreover, There should be certain percentage of marks in the class attendance because it is found that in general education, the students are ignoring the attendance or class teaching which is an essential tool as well as weapon for the students for raising their knowledge, skill and behaviour. If there is marks in the class attendance, the students do not ignore its percentage because the present regulation of 75% class attendance is being proved null and void. College administration and teacher, too, remain in a fix what to do at the time of fulfilling the examination form.

Moreover, the teaching staff of the department must be raised, so that the optimal student-teacher ratio must be maintained. In this context there is sincere role of H.R.D. government of state/union so that with the increase in number of students, post of teacher must be created, appointment must be made. At present, there is a great divergence between student and teacher ratio in each department of college/university.

One of important suggestion for improving the teaching in economics is to create the optimum and modern infrastructure in college before raising the number of seats in honours as well as the general course. In Jharkhand, infact, it is an open door admission policy but for this subject, it is limited one because only meritorious and skillful students opt this subject as the honours one.

## CONCLUSION

In brief we may conclude that the teacher should help to more appropriate design teaching resource/support that will encourage economics teaching at undergraduate level, concept of economic evaluation is an open course designed to teach students how to use economic theory, along with various concepts regarding economic evaluation to conduct economic analysis. Students will study a variety of topic including the application of marginal decision-making various cost benefit models and interpreting and evaluating cost-benefit analysis for determining policy recommendations. Those who complete the course will gain an understanding of basic economic concepts such as cost effectiveness, cost utility, cost of illness and cost minimisation. The course is taught with an eye towards economic evaluation in country, the principles taught may applied to many economic systems. Lectures will be accompanied by problem sets featuring hypothetical real world, economics-based challenges intended to reinforce the theoretical topics covered.

Moreover, the students across the world reading undergraduate degree will find this process of intermingling of theory and real life problems beneficial. "Thus teaching in economics should be integrated with all its subjects such as theory, money banking,international trade, employment finance, Indian economic problems, growth planning and environmental economics, quantitative theory, Demography, Agricultural economics, etc. This would certainly form the solid basis to grow up for higher and again higher study in economics or other branches. It should be incorporated with optimum courses of study student-teacher ratio, examination system and performances. According to our Ex-president, A.P.J. Abdul Kalam. we need the kind of higher education that will create employment opportunities, thus in economics a multi-pronged strategic teaching is required to make education more attractive and simultaneously create employment potential. Hence in economics courses of study, we should add entrepreneurship as one of the paper and prepare students for setting up enterprises which will provided them creativity, freedom and the ability to generate wealth. Thus syllabus should prepared at the undergraduate level in such a way so that the spirit that, "We Can Do it" should be inculcated and for this banks should provide sufficient financial help from village level to prospective entrepreneurs for lunching enterprises. At last the undergraduate syllabus should have the concept of PURA (Providing Urban Amenities in Rural Areas), interlinking of river in cost-benefit approach, Infrastructure missions, Power missions and Tourism. This would certainly be helpful in creating a mature entrepreneurship having a great sense of value to education and value to motivation which are essential for rapid sustainable equitable economic development of this poverty-ridden massive unemployment bonded state like Jharkhand.

## References


An Economists' overview of higher Education", In financing higher Education—COOMBS.

Annual issues of Manorama.

Different admission registers of Madhupur College, Madhupur.

G.D. Sharma and Mridula, Economics of College Education.

Baljit Singh, Economics of Indian Education.

Shyam Kumar Philip, H., Jharkhand—A study.

Syllabus of S.K.M. University, Dumka.

Carter, Allan M., The economics of higher Education: In Contemporary Economic Issues.

Universal Education, Vol. 2.

# Some Reflections on Teaching and Research in Economics

U.N. Choubey and Sharmishtha Priti

In the first decade of 21st century the status of Economics is supreme in Social Sciences and is very close to positive sciences with the increasing role of quantitative method of teaching and research in Economics. With the growing tendency of quantification of knowledge the place of Economics is bound to go up among the different branches of knowledge. Both students and teachers of economics are looked in high esteem on the campus of universities and colleges. During the last 150 years when Mahadeo Govind Ranade was the first student graduate with Economics to this day Economics has passed through several stages. In the beginning its courses of study was limited only to classical economics from Adam Smith to J.S. Mill. There was little scope for quantitative study. Several topics now taught in political Science, Sociology and philosophy were formerly included under the syllabus of Economics. Then came the age of Marshall in the fag end of the 19th Century. It was the period when Economics attracted the students and gradually in all colleges Economics became a popular subject up to pass course standard. With increasing tempo of national movement study of the economic problems of India became popular for people in general and students in particular. Now there was increasing consciousness among people that Economics is a subject directly related to life. It is not only an intellectual exercise.

The crave for the study of Economics increased after soviet Revolution because the whole concept of Socialism needed clarity in the concepts of economic terms. Even among people having not read Economics in their college and university days began to take part in the discussion or economic issues. Great Depression and emergence of Keynes further opened the expanding horizon of Economics. In Indian national movement during thirties socialism and planned economic development became the two important topic of discussion. Now Economics as such became a very import out subject from academic point of view and in almost all universities postgraduate teaching started. The role of professional economists was recognized in solving the economic problems of the country. Dr. V.K.R.V. Rao and Dr. P.C. Mahalanobis were important members of National Planning Committee constituted by Netajee Subash Chandra Bose under the Chairmanship of Pt. Jawaharlal Nehru.

Research facilities also started in several universities in Economics but this facility was limited to a few universities during the pre-independence days. Research facilities in true sense of the term started in the post-independence era not only in the universities but separate research institutes were established both at national and state level. There has been increasing nexus between professional economist and the government bodies. They are included in planning commission and finance commission in different capabilities. They are also included in different committees and commissions related to economic and financial issues.

After the introduction of Economic reform measures Economics is dominating over politics of the country. It is in one way, the recognition of both professional and pragmatic importance of Economics that the professional economist is head of the Government as the Prime Minister. Now economic discussions are limited not only to university campus. They are discussed from parliament to street tea-shop. Under the circumstances it is high time for we professional economists to ponder over teaching and research in Economics so that we could prove more useful and relevant both in enhancing the knowledge horizon of Economics as well as in solving the economic issues the country is facing today.

In the teaching of Economics important issues to be discussed are:

(i) Syllabus;
(ii) Medium of Study;
(iii) Method of teaching;
(iv) Uniformity in teaching;
(v) Number of Students;
(vi) Role of Teachers;
(vii) Extra-curricular Facilities to students;
(viii) Examination and Evaluation; and
(ix) Orientation and Refresher Courses.

In economics today the first and foremost issue is to make the syllabus up to date and relevant to deal with problems which India is facing in the present global world. We also find divergence between courses of study of central universities and state-level universities. This divergence leads to different level-playing causing differences in the quality of products. Now instead of traditional courses teaching of Business Economics, Environmental Economics, Mathematical Economics, Labour Economics and Fiscal Economics are more relevant. The objective of the study should be development-oriented. When we think about development, we have to keep in mind the different dimensions of development. What economists call 'development', political Scientists call 'modernisation', Sociologists call, 'Role differentiation' and Anthropologists call 'Culture change'. Certainly economis is an engine of progress and paves the way for human and social welfare. The syllabus should be re-framed in this light and old and traditional topics be replaced by modern and relevant topics in the context of present global world. The feet of modern Economics is not in politics or philosophy but in the basic foundation of positive science while the head is in the objectives of welfare to society and humanity.

The question of medium of instruction of Economics is a matter of great concern. Many state level universities have started teaching Economics in Hindi or in their state languages.

Economics is the subject whose roast are in foreign land. All standard text books are in English. Students either depend on cheap books written in Hindi or in vernacular languages or on the translation of foreign books. It causes difficulties in the clarity or conceptual anaysis and in proper understanding of the topic. At the national level in Seminars and conferences we find that both students and teachers of Hindi-speaking states participate but feel shy in expressing their views in English. Virtually they become back bench sitters and suffer from inferiority complex. So, only students having excellence in English language should be encouraged to study economics. The medium of teaching of Economics also should be English from graduate level itself. This will bring self-confidence among the students and they will comprehend the subject in full originality and entirity. It will reduce the gulf between the urban and rural, national and regional level of teaching as well as reading of Economics.

Presently only two methods of teaching are popular in Economics (i) Lecturer method, (ii) Notes dictating method. Lecture method is old and traditional method. It has become out of date and bearing for the student of Economics. Economics is a lively subject. It is both abstract and concrete. Therefore, mere lecture by a teacher is not so fruitful. Dictating notes is the symbol of deteriorating standard of teaching. Through this methods, students may fetch goods marks at the examinations but they will lack conceptual clarity of Economic theories and terms. Teaching Economics should be through interaction method. It will make the class room lively. It will be more light-giving and fruit-bearing. Abstract economic theories should be taught with concrete examples of every day life because Economics in the combination of both abstractions and pragmatism.

Uniformity in teaching is very essential. It is the lack of uniformity that we find a great difference between the mental up gradation of students of national universities and rural-based colleges. Rural-based colleges also should be equipped with infrastructural facilities and reading materials as are the colleges of central universities. For postgraduate classes improved libraries, computers with internet facilities and standard magazines and journals are pre-requisites. It is a sad commentary on the part of teaching in Economics that in recent years the number of students reading economics is declining. The possibility of finding job for a well-equipped student of Economics is more than any discipline of knowledge. The onus goes on the teaching fraternity to make the students know the different avenues that economics provides to the young in making their career bright. Teachers should also be a little liberal in marking while evaluating Answer Books. Traditionally examiners in economics are known for their conservative approach.

The role of teachers in teaching Economics is of paramount of importance. The body language of teacher of Economics should be quite distinguishing. Economics is a developing subject. So, teachers have to be regular in updating their knowledge through the study of recently published books, journals and attending Seminars, symposium and conferences of Economics. He should equip himself both in abstract theories and problems of real Economics facing the economy in the era of liberalisation and globalisation. In the classroom teachers has to be always conscious to the fact that students are attentive. It is possible only when students find useful facts in the lecture of the teacher. It is sad that most of the teachers go to the class unprepared and engage the classes in a casual manner. It is also one of the reason that the students are indifferent to attend classes and the percentage of absentee students is increasing day-by-day. The role and character of the teachers should he such as to inculcate moral and ethical value among students. The commercial attitude of teachers in general and in Economics in particular is responsible for the deteriorating respect of teachers in society in general and among the students in particular.

The teaching of Economics cannot be limited to class room. The students of Economics should get magazines, journals, Internet facilities, good library and opportunity to participate in Seminars and symposium. They should get the facility of excursion to visit places of economic importance and also big factories and business places. The present system of examination and evaluation is traditional, out of date and purposeless. The questions are set on traditional pattern which are easily guessed and students depend upon guess papers for their examinations. They do not study text books. Questions should be such that students should go through whole text book. Moreover, there should be more terminal examinations and some marks should be allotted for terminal examinations also.

The topics of orientation courses and refresher courses should be revised and provision be made to include all categories of teachers to participate in such courses. There should be no age bar. Refresher Course in quantitative Economics is must for all universities. Old teachers are not trained in quantitative method of study. It is a recent trend. Now the need is for every teacher to be well-versed in quantitative method of teaching and the topics of mathematical Economics. The days are gone when mathematical analysis was in the appendix of a book today mathematical analysis constitute the heart of a book and micro and macroeconomics and in 90% articles in any standard journal mathematical models have been frequently used. It is why we find many teachers indifferent to study such books and journals. Such teachers are expected to labour a bit more for some time to get themselves trained in mathematical economics.

So far reach in Economics is concerned, there are several constraints and handicaps. Constraints at college-level are more than at university-level. Till the 10th Plan, research was considered as the growing prerogative of universities. The method of registration is so clumsy that college teachers are discouraged. A college teacher has to take more classes and he has to spend more time in family affairs with growing children. They do not find involve for in research projects which demand discipline, unlimited time, persistence and passion to work at all stages of research project cycle. It is enough for them to teach and be at home and not do anything else about academics throughout their career. They become complacent. Ideas do not blossom from senior faculty due to monotonous, repeated lectures for years. Senior teachers think that they know everything of curriculum and teach without updating till retirement. There are many teachers of Economics who do not even deliver lectures but spend their whole teaching tenure in dictating notes for the students to learn by-heart and replica in the examinations. Most of the colleges and universities are bogged down by vernacular languages and incapable to produce even a research paper. Moreover, applying for a research project in English and succeeding to get the project grant is very formidable task for this faculty in both colleges and universities. Now in most of the universities, time bound promotion scheme has been implemented. So, teachers do not find incentive for research pursuits. College teachers also fear that they cannot complete research project. They consider it the prerogatives of university teachers. It is also true that most of the college lack improved library, computers with internet facilities and other physical and human infrastructure to complete research projects. They also lack fund. UGC fund is usually usurped by the teachers of the colleges and universities adjacent to Delhi. Research institutes approved centre for research do not readily support, collaborate and network with college teachers. There is an air of pseudo superiority when they deal with college faculty.

In a survey by UNESCO, 52% college teachers admitted that they are not doing research together with teaching. 68% admitted that they feel difficulty to manage teaching and research 16% wanted to pursue research but lacked fund 52% did not find administrative support to complete research. Today universities and colleges are gradually turning as teaching shops and research is considered the monopoly of the institutions which have been established for research only. No doubt, UGC is trying its best to inculcate research spirit in the teaching fraternity of higher education. XIth plan document UGC grants extended to teachers of colleges and Universities for minor and major research project. Commission approved 96 major research projects in Humanities and Social Sciences this year. College faculty members are required to do two refresher courses at research institutes or Academic staff college required for promotions so that they are exposed to research institutions during refresher courses. Principals of colleges are required to be Ph.D. degree holders so that they could know importance of research for academic only by providing research facilities to college teachers we can dream of achieving quality education for all subjects in general and for Economics in particular.

Discrimination between college teachers and university teachers for research funding should be to totally removed. Criteria-based evaluation of proposals for funding research should be adopted procedures for research funding should be more transparent. Taking up research projects should be made not only compulsory for promotion in Economics but also should be made an eligibility criteria on to be employed as teacher. Each college should be encouraged to develop a research centre with its own vision.

A teacher in teaching should not only be a teacher but also play the role of facilitator and counselor as guide and supervisor of research scholars. There should be a linkage between university and industry. University and corporate sector for improving teaching skills through practical knowledge as per need and requirement of papers taught by the teachers in Economics. Economics is having multi-disciplinary approach. Therefore, Economics students should have knowledge about quantitative techniques. Teaching becomes lively only when are talks of applications of economics, thus, it is very helpful to explain the practical application of economics, in business decision-making. Market as well institution must encourage right-type of students in Economics by providing job-assurance and placement as well as by offering scholarships. Continuous dialogue among the teachers of Economics is necessary regarding teaching methodology; curriculum, etc. It is also necessary to have an exchange of sharing experiences and experiments in teaching of economics with the country and abroad too. Examination-oriented teaching need to enhance knowledge-oriented so as to fulfil expectation and aspirations of society and government.

In recent years research in Economics has become popular at college, University and Institute-level but the quality of research has deteriorated. Students are enrolled in research without considering their talent and skill to pursue research projects. At university-level, there are complaints of manipulative degrees and turning research cell as milky cow for commercial guides and university officials. Every year research scandals are published in the Newspaper in one university or the other. As such it is very essential that a scholar must go to study Methodologies in research in the institute where such type of training courses are organized. With increasing importance of quantitative techniques every student who wants to be registered for research degree, must be given training of fundamentals of quantitative technique. To make the research more fruitful research projects based upon primary sources of data should be promoted. It should always be kept in mind that Ph.D. degree is not the end of research. It is just a stepping-stone for higher study. The Guide must be specialist of the topic. It is a bad convention that scholars of multi-dimensions are registered under the same guide. Every care has to be taken that the degree is not manipulative or pampered. Only then teachers and students of economics can play their vital role in the acceleration of the pale of Economic development of the country.

To sum of the discussion, Economics is developing social science. So, constant evaluation is required to provide desired level of teaching; talented and skilled manpower and quality research with innovations and experimentations. Economics has to face the challenges of 21st century in the era of liberalisation and globalisation. Economics has world to win and establish itself at the top of all other subjects showing the ways for amelioration of poverty and unemployment and usher is prosperity of whole mankind.

## References


Blangh, E.D. (1971), Economics of Education, Vol. 2, Harmonds Wata, Penguin Books.

Dave, H.L. (2005), Teaching of Economics, 35th Annual Conference of GEA, Bhrauch.

Dhand (1990), Techniques of Teaching, Ashish Publication House, New Delhi.

Dr. Siddique, M.N. (1993), Teaching of Economics, Ashish Publication House, New Delhi.

Kurien, C.T. (2001), Towards more Relevant Teaching of Economics; Malcom Adiseshaiah Memorial Lecturer of 84th Conference of IEA, Vellore.

Mohanty, Laxman (2002), Innovation in Teaching, *University News*: 40(31); August 5-11.

Pillai, V.R. (1962), Reflection on Teaching in Economics in India: Presidential Address, IEA Conference, Ahmedabad.

Srinivasan, M.V. (2008), Teaching Economics, A comment, *EPW*, Oct. 18, 2008.

Sukhmoy Chakravarty (1987), The Teaching of Economics of India, Himalaya Publication House, Mumbai.

UNESCO, Forum on Higher Education, Resarch and Knowledge, Scon Colloquium on Resarch and Higher Education Policy held between 29 Nov.-1st December, 2006.

Vedanayatma, G. (1988), Teaching Technology for College Teachers, Sterling Publication Pvt. Ltd., Delhi.

# Teaching of Economics at Undergraduate Level

## With Special Reference to Indian Economics

V. LOGANATHAN

## INTRODUCTION

An attempt has been made in this paper to describe and analyse the teaching of Economics at the undergraduate level with special reference to Indian Economics. To begin with, the paper discusses the present status of the teaching of economics in general. After discussing the objectives of teaching economics at undergraduate level, it describes the general criticism against the content and method(s) of teaching economics. Next, it goes on to explain the meaning of *Indian Economics* and analyses the views of different schools of thought. It concludes by pointing out the irrelevance of some of the western techniques of thinking and the analytical tools applied to study the Indian economic problems and solutions offered and points out the need for constructing relevant tools of analysis.

## Teaching of Economics

In the new millennium, the world faces a "trilemma" of balancing international economic integration, the nation-state, and mass politics in the next 100 years. There are some who forecast that nation-states will give way to global federalism.

The primary goal of any course in economics should be to enable students to think like economists. The teaching should help students to develop and exercise their critical thinking. But even many teachers of economics have beliefs about economics that are more highly correlated with those of journalists than with those of economists. So there is need for a greater use and appreciation of economic analysis.

The main objectives set forth for an undergraduate economics course are: to help students have an understanding of (a) basic economic problems, (b) national and international economic institutions under which the domestic economy functions in a global framework, (c) the structure of Indian economy—resource ownership, production system, market and the State, etc., and (d) exposure to basic economic theories and their application to current economic problems (Srinivasan, R., 2002).

The major complaints of students and faculty against the teaching of economics are: insufficient emphasis given to real-world problems and to empirical applications and policy issues, excessive emphasis on mathematical technique for its own sake, narrowness of content, lack of attention to economic history and the need for more history of thought and interdisciplinary knowledge (W. Lee Hansen).

We may, however, note that even serious economic analysis can be presented without burdening the student with mathematics. For example, Irving Fisher's style of teaching was: "Say it in words, demonstrate it in graphs and tables, and if technical details are needed, place them in appendices or provide references."

Twentieth century economics generally was called "neoclassical economics." Keynes was of the view: "The study of economics does not seem to require any specialised gifts of an unusually high order. Is it not, intellectually regarded, a very easy subject compared with the higher branches of philosophy and pure science? Yet good, or even competent economists are the rarest of birds. An easy subject at which very few excel."

By 2000, there was a fundamental change in the economics profession, and in the modern study of the history of economic thought, we often use 2000 as the end of the neoclassical era and the beginning of the New Millennium Era (The term New Millennium Economics was used by Colander in 2000).

Solow described the economics of the 1990s as a collection of analytical tools to be applied quite directly to observable situations. The shift in emphasis from the 1940s to the 1990s did not occur suddenly. It occurred slowly over the period as older economists retired and younger ones came in. What distinguished the economics of the late 1990s was not formalism *per se*. While the economic models of the 1990s often contained a hearty dose of mathematics, the mathematics itself was never deep.... The key component of the economics in the late 1990s was "model building." In graduate schools in U.S., students didn't learn much about actual institutions or problems; instead, they all learned the same set of analytic models, which they then applied directly to reality. Solow attributed the spread of model-building to several factors: the problems the older discursive approach had with maintaining objectivity, the demand of policy-makers for quantitative answers, and the fact that even the primitive computers of that time had produced an increased availability of data and the greater ease of analyzing that data.

New millennium economists still use models, but they are quite different models than the deductive models of the 1990s that Solow described. Modern models are more like weather models in the late 1990s. These new models come to many of the same conclusions as the old models; economists still believe price incentives are important and that markets solve coordination problems, but that belief is not held with the almost religious conviction with which it was held in the neoclassical era.

Specifically, New Millennium economics does rot base policy on the neoclassical welfare theorems (which were part of its broader "right price" view of the policy). That view of policy has been replaced by our current "right institutions" view of policy.

## Teaching of Indian Economics

Nearly a century ago, our national leaders like Lala Lajpat Rai, Gopalkrishna Gokhale and Netaji Subhash Chandra Bose identified our chief national problems as follows:

1. Eradication of poverty,
2. Eradication of Illiteracy,
3. Eradication of disease, and
4. Scientific production and distribution.

1. Netaji believed that the above problems could be tackled only along socialist lines. Because, distribution gets priority only in a socialist agenda.

On accepting the Nobel Prize in Economics in 1979, Theodore W. Schultz said: "Most of the people in the world are poor; so if we knew the economics of being poor, we would know much of the economics that matters." While Adam Smith considered economics as an enquiry into the wealth of nations, Myrdal looked at it as the study of the causes of the poverty of nations. The latter was largely writing about India in his *Asian Drama* (1968).

To make the teaching of economics effective, it is necessary to realize that Indian economy is characterized by a considerable extent of structural heterogeneity: "exclusive emphasis on neoclassical "price economics" is, therefore, likely to prove seriously misleading if the student is to understand better the process of allocation, growth and distribution. This is not to argue that elementary laws of demand and supply do not apply in India. What it means is that to understand the operation of these forces, one must clearly comprehend the structural features of the Indian economy. Traditional price theory does not apply here because there are no uniform markets for labour, capital (and even commodities) because of the absence of mobility and the very considerable requirements of 'search costs' which are implied in the rule of 'one price for one commodity'.

There is need for teaching the social circulation of commodities and services in the beginning itself. The input-output analysis in the broad sense, going back to Quesnay, deserves to be put at the centre of teaching, along with suitable consideration of all relevant factors shaping final demand components. The role of institutions as analyzed by Veblen should not be neglected. As the input-output coefficients change, largely because of technological change, a study of factors shaping technological change deserves a prominent place in our curriculum. A study of economic history can also become an essential part of our teaching programme. There is also a need for linking sociology of development with what we teach under development economics.

K.N. Raj and Sukhamoy Chakravarty believed that the study of the Indian economy should be one of the major foci of economics teaching in India and felt sad that It is here that one encountered serious shortfalls in teaching. Prof. Chakravarthy asks: "Why has the teaching of the subject which attracts some of the very best minds taken such a fragmentary form, when what is probably most needed is to impart a knowledge of Indian economic life and organisation. There is a big hiatus between what is taught in the classroom and what obtains outside. Bridging this gap is probably one of the major problems of teaching economics in India.

It is true that excellent articles have appeared in *Economic and Political Weekly* by great economists. But the fact remains that the outcome of these researches has not found its place in the mainstream of undergraduate and postgraduate teaching in India. A lot of methodological insights could also be gained from some of these contributions. But they should form part of the teaching of theory, techniques and tools.

It may be of interest to note that the major findings of the Nobel Laureates in Economics have found their way into the undergraduate text books in the US.

The Social Framework of J.R. Hicks is a good introduction to the U.K. economy. But to understand village India, a different or modified social framework is needed. It is a challenging and creative work.

John Kenneth Galbraith (1962) lamented: "As an economist, I look with considerable discontent on much of the economics that is taught in the new countries. It is not clinically concerned with the problems of their countries and pragmatically with their solutions."

According to Sukhamoy Chakravarthy, the problem of teaching of economics in India divides into three parts; what we teach, how we teach and what should be taught. In the past, there were only a couple of papers which were devoted to the study of Indian economic problems. As he put it, "This is partly history, partly description and partly a discussion of current policy issues. These papers often bear a tenuous relationship to what is taught under the heading of 'micro' and 'macroeconomics' which constitute the basic contents of the papers on the theory.

**Economics and Developing Countries**

The difficulties in explaining economic development of developing countries are greater than in the case of economic growth, as institutional and structural changes play an important role in the former. Many economic problems of less developed countries can be successfully tackled only if their social and institutional setting is transformed. A satisfactory theory of economic development can only be evolved in an interdisciplinary setting. In the narrow economic field, concepts and theories appropriate to developed capitalist countries are carelessly applied to the less developed countries (LDCs) without bearing in mind, the basic differences in circumstances which have a great bearing on their applicability.

*To cite a few examples*

(1) The capital-output ratio is often used as a planning tool in developing countries. In its emphasis on one factor as determining economic progress, it reminds one of the faith of the physiocrats in land. For, one runs the risk of what Myrdal calls the logical fallacy of illegitimate isolation. If all other prerequisites of growth are easily available, then savings can be mobilised and turned into investment goods. Then the assumption is valid. While it is legitimate to assume that unskilled labour supply is infinitely elastic even in the short-run, we cannot say the same thing of skilled labour, management or credit.

(2) The economic theory received from the West has failed to explain the prevalent income distribution. This arises mainly from the fact that it has missed the pervasive and preventable causes of economic inequality, the unequal distribution of ownership and the natural disadvantages and handicap of birth and upbringing under conditions of extreme poverty. There is a further disadvantage in the computation of income in developing countries. Income distribution

is often thought of in terms of remuneration to factors of production like land, labour and capital according to their marginal productivity, but when the predominant number of persons are self-employed, the significance of these explanatory categories is much less. Another important factor is that in economics where there are grave bottlenecks to mobility of labour and capital, and where availability of economic structure and access to information and technology are very different, factors command different rewards depending on where they work.

(3) In a country where a large number of persons are below the poverty line, increase in certain types of consumption become as essential as investment for future increase in national income; essential consumption may help development more than non-priority investment. In such cases, the distinction between consumption and saving as two exclusive categories, one to be restrained and the other to be encouraged, become an example of illegitimate isolation.

(4) Since 1960s, economists have realised the importance of investment in human capital. Expenditure on education has been recognized as a very valuable form of investment deserving high priority. But in the LDCs, the western type of liberal education which has attracted a large number of students, has often proved socially unproductive and led to substantial increase in educated unemployment,

(5) The unemployment problem in the LDCs is different from that in the developed economies. We cannot explain the problem of unemployment in LDCs in terms of lack of effective demand or wage rigidity due to the strength of the trade unions. There is a great difference in the impact of deficit financing in the two contexts. Secondly, because of the problem of disguised unemployment and seasonal unemployment in agriculture, it becomes difficult to measure unemployment by a distinct figure as in developed countries. Countries have developed at

different times in different institutional settings and historical circumstances. Thus Great Britain developed under *laissez faire*.

Germany and France under protectionism and interlinking of banking with industry. The USA had the advantage of size and unexplored resources. Japan had the benefit of a competitively isolated economy and state-led capitalism combined with strongly oligopolistic private capitalists to get over the initial obstacles to growth. The U.S.S.R. developed under a system of socialism and centralised planning.

**The Evolution of Economic Thinking in India**

Over the last one hundred years, Indian economists have written at length and on many topics. Besides these writings, there have also been numerous Committees and Commissions whose reports have led to a voluminous literature. In a rough way, we may say that there were two schools of thought. One school felt that as the Indian institutions, customs and modes of thought and reactions were so different from the Western ones that the economic theory evolved in the West was inapplicable to India. The argument was strengthened by appealing to the unique Indian institutions like caste, joint family, the deeply religious and custom-bound and tradition-oriented nature of the people and the isolated and self-sufficient character of the agricultural economy and rural industry. This was essentially the thinking behind the phrase *"Indian Economics"* (The basic idea in this connection was worked out by M.G. Ranade in *" Essays on Indian Economics": A collection of Essays and Speeches,* Madras, 1920). But suitable models for India were not evolved and Indian economics became largely factual and descriptive. The continental size and variety of the Indian economy presented a considerable obstacle to its comprehension; and simple models like those of export economies furnished no help in understanding it. Facts on the Indian economy were few and covered a small sector. This was specially so when a regional break-up was attempted, or where a comparative picture over time was drawn, without which few deductions were possible.

The other group of scholars, who were deeply impressed by the Western thought stressed the universality of economic laws.

Dr. Bhabatosh Dutta in his *"The Evolution of Economic Thinking in India"* makes the point that one major reason why economists endowed with the speculative capacity of the Indian mind, did not distinguish themselves in the realm of economic theory as they should have, was that besides being preoccupied with current problems, they wrongly found readymade western economic theory satisfactory. While many economists of the second school of thought recognized the great differences between the Indian and western backgrounds, they either dismissed them as a passing phenomenon or mere temporary aberrations, which were only due to foreign rule or would disappear with development. Dadabhai Naoroji with his penetrating analysis of poverty and of the drain theory may be regarded as typical of this school.

There was a third school of thought which emphasized a thorough historic analysis of economic reality. R.C. Dutt was the pioneer of this school of thought.

Indian economists, in general, have emphasized the role of the State compared with the *laisseze faire* policy advocated by the British and the foreign economists.

### The Search for Relevance and the Need for a Separate Analytical Framework

There are some economists who believe that we must have a separate analytical framework for analyzing the problems of the Indian economy. To quote, "It will be the task of Indian economics to build up an independent analytical framework for analyzing the problems of the Indian economy. It begins with the search for the operational concepts that will more satisfactorily than before help in understanding the structure and functioning of the Indian economic system. Relentless scrutiny of structure and hypotheses borrowed from western economic analysis must get the highest priority. In fact, this has been done on a good scale by Indian economists. These separate critiques, however, have not been brought together to form coherent framework for further analysis. Also, all these have been in a sense, negative. What does not work or signify has been noted but what will has not been specified or suggested. What is also lacking is a more detailed study of social, economic and political institutions in India to broadly sketch the background and the factors that may be significant for economic analysis of Indian conditions. Many fellow economists with whom I have had the opportunity of discussing this problem do not find it difficult to accept the principle of relativity of economic theory but seem reluctant to take the next logical step and accept Indian economics as an independent discipline. On further probing, one discovers that this stems from the fear of the unknown. If there is no general economic theory, then in studying Indian economic problems, we are at sea without rudder or compass. If there is no analytical frame, how do we proceed? What are we supposed to analyse with? (N.V. Somani, 1974).

Professor Malcolm S. Adiseshiah, in his presidential. Address to the 57th Annual Conference of the Indian Economic Association has made the following suggestion with regard to the teaching of Economics.

"With regard to economics teaching the start could be a fairly thorough grounding in the Indian institutional frame; the next stage would be the study of the theoretical concepts which have emerged in the affluent economies, both capitalist and socialist, and which apply fairly fully to them... The purpose of this second stage is to help in understanding the economic tools as they have grown out of their environment as well; as in the methodological rigour that all science learning calls for, the third stage is the most difficult stage, it is yet to be worked out, and that is the theory frames and concepts that will be arising out of the study of our economy. A fourth and final stage would be a study of the history of Indian economic thought. This is probably an even more difficult exercise than stage three because, as far as I know no connected, continuous attempt has been made to identify the work and conceptual contributions of Indian economists", Prof. C.T. Kurien, in his *Poverty, Planning and Social Transformation* (1978) developed a conceptual frame to study the interaction of the structure and the working of the Indian economy.

In the 70s, at the international level, there was a shift of emphasis in the discussion on the problem of development. As against the practice in the 50s and 60s of identifying development with growth, and of expressing growth as an aggregate figure, the discussion in the seventies called for a more disaggregated approach. Along with it came the recognition that if development was concerned basically with improving the quality of life of the vast majority of people, growth alone was not sufficient, and that creation of employment opportunities and deliberate redistributive measures were required to achieve the objective (C.T. Kurien). "The questions to be asked about a country's development are: What has been happening to poverty? What has been happening to unemployment? What has been happening to inequality? If all the three have been declined from high levels then beyond doubt this has been a period of development for the country. If they have worsened, it would be strange to call the result 'development' even if per capita income doubled." (Dudley Seers, 1969).

There was disenchantment with industrialisation as a means to growth. And there was also the realisation that traditional agriculture in the LDCs could be transformed through technology and modern farming practices. As Prof. Kurien put it, "Rural Development" suddenly moved into the centre of development dialogue and leading institutions like the World Bank became the champion of the cause.

First came the Green Revolution and then a number of special schemes for rural development. Since 1976, *Integrated Rural Development* became the official policy in the country.

## CONCLUSION

We may conclude by saying that the task facing the economist in India is not so much of rejecting the irrelevant as of constructing the relevant.

### REFERENCES

Chakravarty, Sukhamoy co-authored with Jagdish Bhagwati, 1969. 'Contributions to Indian Economic Analysis: A survey, *American Economic Review*, September 1959, Part 2, Supplement): 2-73. Reprinted in 1971, New Delhi, Lalwani Publishing House.

Dadabhai Naoroji, Poverty and Un-British Rule in India, Delhi, 1962.

Dudley Seers, Paper presented at the 11th World Conference of the Society for International Development, New Delhi, 1969, p. 3.

Ganguli, B.N., Indian Economic Thought: Nineteenth Century Perspectives, Tata McGraw-Hill, New Delhi, 1977.

Gunnar Myrdal, Asian Drama, An Inquiry into the Poverty of Nations, The Benquin Press, 1968.

John Kenneth Galbraith in his "Economic Development in Perspective", (1962).

Kurien, C.T., Poverty, Planning and Social Transformation, Allied Publishers, 1978.

Lee Hansen W. cited in Janet T. Knoedles, Daniel, A. Underwood, Teaching principles of economics: A proposal for a Multi-paradigmatic Approach, AFIT Roundtable in Pedagogy in Principles of Economics (1998).

Somani, N.V, "Indian Economics and Indian Economists", *Indian Economic Journal*, 21(3), January-March 1974.

Srinivasan, R. (2002): "The State of Undergraduate Economics Courses in Tamil Nadu University" in *Review of Development and Change*, Vol.VII, No. 2, pp. 363-85.

# The Economics of Defence

## Need to Argument Research

A.P. Tiwari

## INTRODUCTION

The application of economics to national defence is a relatively new branch of discipline. The problem of relative worths and costs of quality and quantity in both military and private industry is an economic problem which is amenable to economic calculus. Significantly, a considerable amount of world's resources are mobilised for defence budget—about $ 1,464 billion in 2008. The share of the US was $ 607 billion accounting 41.5 per cent of the world total. Defence expenditure comprised 2.4 per cent of world GDP in 2008. Interestingly, if the US defence spending is excluded, the rest of the world spends 1.85 per cent of GDP. Indian defence spending stood at $ 30 billion in 2008. This calculates at about 3 per cent of GDP. India with 2.1 per cent share occupies 10th position in the world list of defence spending. But our knowledge of defence economics is so scant that we do not even have an accepted definition of 'defence output'. However, defence output may be expressed in terms of 'military effectiveness' and 'optimum defence output' as 'maximum military effectiveness' implying 'maximum annihilation of enemy nation at minimum cost'. Countries try to increase their security by raising their defence spending. However, it is paradoxical that humanity is increasingly becoming more insecure than what it was earlier. The increasing costs of defence is not necessarily being accepted fatalistically by those countries that occupy dominant position in their share of world defence spending. Moreover, the economic effects of defence spending are enormous and complex. In fact, defence spending involves huge opportunity costs. Despite deep and wide existence of defence-development spin-offs, the realm remains less-researched. In view of this, this paper revisits into some core analytics and empirics of defence economics. The paper focuses on the need to augment both theoretical and empirical research on various dimensions of the economics of defence. Whatever may be the views of different thinkers on the budget level of defence effectiveness, they should have a common interest in efficient allocation. The issue of 'how much defence spending is enough?' leads us beyond the boundaries of economics. Hence, an inter-disciplinary research on the economics of defence may be an agreeable idea.

**The Analytics**

An enquiry into the fiscal dynamics of Indian defence leads us to infer that the three major defence crises which had to be faced during the decade 1962-72 have had profound impact on the public finances of the country and thereby influenced significantly the patterns and priorities of Plan and non-Plan spending of the Central and State Governments, especially of the former. Combined with other crises the fiscal pressures from the side of defence have at times produced intense and lasting effects upon the fiscal capacity of the country, as for instance witnessed in the compulsion to postpone launching of the Fourth Five Year Plan and thus causing an irreparable breach in the initially conceived long-run strategy of economic development. Similarly, the large deficits in the Central budgets during the middle and latter years of the Fourth Five Year Plan have in no small measures been due to the pre-occupation of the eastern wing of Pakistan. In so far as maintenance of sound defence potential is the responsibility of the government, its responses to periodically emerging defence crises have caused diversions of spending from non-defence to defence sector and more meaningfully a restructuring of Plan and non-Plan coordination.

The advances in military technology even in relation to conventional wars and small powers have caused the financial cost of defence to become uncertain and in the absence of a long-terms strategic doctrine, as also in the absence of a continuous implementation of a long-term strategy of economic development, have made it appear to the government as something which is uncontrollable, and which cannot, thus, be adequately provided for in advance. At least, this has been the posture presented to the public in the budget speeches of the Finance Minister. Acceleration of inflationary tendencies caused by increasing over-all deficits in the Central budgets have conveniently been made, *inter alia*, the direct product of defence-uncertainties. It may well be argued, however, that a little different alignments in the material and financial balances of the Plan, might not have produced the same measure of dis-equilibrium in the finances, money supply and prices.

While it is true that in general defence and development go together and the absence of a clash between the two was appreciated as early as in the wake of the Indo-Chinese War, what has not been true is the fact that the real physical requirements of defence enterprises were not built-up into the input-output matrices of the Plan-making processes with the result that both the physical and financial impact of emergent crises appeared with heightened suddenness and caused bewilderment to those charged with managing the country's finances and raising of financial resources for the execution of the Five Year Plans. Post-Pokhran and post-Kargil security perspectives have enhanced the paramountcy of research on Indian defence economics with special focus on exploring trade-offs between defence and civilian sectors. It would be relevant here to discuss some of the analytics of defence economics in international perspective. The focus is on discussing the fiscal dynamics of defence.

Review of the economics of defence leads us to conclude that an important phase in the development of economic ideas about defence began with the appearance of large-scale military establishments in the major European powers. The two World Wars and the intervening years produced a great deal of economic comment on defence and military power. But these were pre-

Keynesian times and the economics of national management were not yet agreed upon. Thus much of the discussion, while possibly morally sound, was at the same time hopelessly wrong in its economic aspects. This was not necessarily the fault of the economists; they were given problems to solve without the means to do so and in conditions where the sheer magnitude of events was beyond anything that the world had experienced up to that time.

Up to the First World War military matters were still considered the exclusive province of the military. If the country fielded a military force that force would get on with the job and settle the issue in the traditional manner. The First World War brought out the relevant connection between military power and the industrial system: without the latter the former was meaningless, for whichever side could sustain the largest force and weight of armaments would be the side that would, if not win, at least be last on its feet. In the years before the Second World War several economists turned their attention to the problems of a war effort and the military leaders were less unprepared for the realities of total conflict than they had been in 1914. One prolific contributor to the discussion was F.W. Hirst, editor of *The Economist.* He was a little-known figure but at the time he wrote widely and clearly about the issues raised by modern war. His views also underwent a slight shift under the actual experience of the First World War. In 1911 he addressed the Manchester Statistical Society and enunciated three principles of war finance, related to Britain. His first principle was that in the economic sense, all expenditures on armies, navies and weapons of destruction is wasteful. This was qualified by his second principle that until universal and perpetual peace has been established some expenditures on their service is absolutely necessary. This was in line with Adam Smith's view that while soldiers were unproductive (in the sense that they did not create productive capital) they were necessary to protect the country from invasion. Hirst's third principle extended the necessity principle into a definition of necessity that preserved that *status quo*. Our expenditure must be sufficient to maintain the Empire, and to give us ample security against invasion. At the same time all excessive and provocative expenditure should be avoided and suppressed. A real effort should be made to secure a proportional limitation of armaments and there should be a severe financial supervision to make sure that the taxpayer gets full value for his money. This theme, in different countries, and on different platforms, has been the standard one of the modern age. With the exclusion of the word 'Empire' the same three principles could appear in any of a dozen political leaders' speeches. Hirst's next development was to become alarmed at the provocative cost of modern armies and war efforts exemplified by the First World War. He published his Political Economy of War in 1914.

Hirst collected the statistics of the arms race between the major powers. He opined that by no possibility could expenditure on this colossal scale be reproductive. It exhausts the sources of national revenues, increases taxation, paralyses the action of national finance and commerce and arrests the general well-being. From this he stated there were three fallacies of war, namely that it had many economic advantages, that it increased wealth, and that it was good for trade. Like the classical economists he had to reconcile the waste of war with the economic prosperity that came with it. His conclusion was that war prosperity was a fictitious stimulus to activity because once the stimulus was withdrawn an augmented quantity of labour is left to compete in the market with greatly diminished quantity of capital.

In the decades after the Second World War the wheel has turned full circle in many ways. The mass unemployment that followed the First World War was not experienced again. The share of the government in the economy had grown enormously. So had the military budgets of the industrialised countries. War prosperity was followed by even greater peacetime prosperity. The use of Keynesian-type fiscal controls meant that a government could effectively choose the broad level of output in the economy. But the growth in government intervention and the sheer size of the resources under government control created a management problem on the one hand and a competitive allocation problem on the other. The competing ends in modern economies have produced over-loaded activity which has resulted in inflation. The government is faced with a problem of how to ensure that the 'tax payer is getting value for his money' (because voting taxpayers have aspirations for alternative uses of their incomes and they resent waste in government expenditure if it means higher taxes than necessary) and the parallel problems of shifting resources to relatively higher valued social activity, such as from defence to welfare. Thus, in the 1960s a new interest in the economics of public management developed and alongside this there was a substantial movement of economists, at least in the American government service, towards tackling defence management problems. At the unofficial level many more economists took up the issues raised by the massive military budgets and researched into the problems of disarmament. Smith's view that defence is a necessity and should be done efficiently is probably still the mainstream one. Its counterpart, that war is so wasteful, and in the nuclear age so dangerous, that alternative means of settling disputes must be found and funded, is supported by a respectable minority.

The unanimously accepted principle of war finance is that once the task of converting productive resources to defence production starts, the various methods of financing defence efforts involve the basic element of coercion to be exercised on civilian consumption. To the extent the civilian consumption is not restricted by various fiscal tools like taxation, borrowing and rationing, consumers are compelled to reduce their purchases to that amount of goods which is left after the defence requirements have been met. Alternative fiscal policies have little effect upon the resources available for the war effort. The latter is a question of materials and manpower—not of finance. Alternative fiscal policies, however, play a vital role by affecting the distribution of the burden of war among the different sections of population. Moreover, it is an undeniable fact that different fiscal policies are capable of creating different psychological atmospheres which consequently have lasting effects on the over-all economic activity. More importantly, in conjunction with the manner in which the war burden is distributed among different sections, this becomes potentially powerful factor by which the productivity and the morale of the people are affected. From the foregoing analysis a major result which emerges is that apart from the positive function of war finance (distribution of burden of war) a negative function call for the avoidance of any policy objective which may impede the strategy of solving real problems connected with the mobilisation of manpower and materials. Thus, the task of fiscal policy in war becomes to see that nothing is decided on fiscal ground.

Fiscal policies, i.e. policies designed to produce means of payment for defence effort consist of either loans or taxes. Rationing is used as a tool to restrict civilian consumption but is not productive of revenue. However, saving resulting from voluntary abstinence or induced by rationing, can easily be transformed into loans, and it makes little difference whether the government receives them directly or permits the banks to create a corresponding amount of purchasing power, as long as borrowing from banks is limited to the amount currently saved by the people. If the amount of government revenue obtained through taxes and loans exceeds current savings, spending of the excess is inflationary in the sense that higher prices reduce consumption to the extent required by the conversion of productive resources to war production. Inflation may automatically play a major role in closing any gap between the required reduction of consumption and such reduction of consumption as is brought about by means of voluntary saving and taxation. The gap is thus always closed in part by means of the orderly and deliberate processes of voluntary saving and taxation, in part by inflation. If savings are defined to include 'forced saving' (through taxation and inflation) savings always suffice to secure such war production as has been ordered.

The financing of war through creation of new money and bank credits, after it has been carried on a certain distance, is liable to generate not merely a progressive but a rapidly accelerating rise of prices. Consequently, the problem of inflation becomes more complicated and acute. Because of the rise in prices, high money wage rates are demanded, this makes price rise still further and so on cumulatively. If the use of this method of war finance is kept within fairly narrow bounds the confidence of public reposed in the currency need not be shaken and the inflationary pressure need not be heightened. But if the method is carried too far by the government, whether through incompetence or through the sheer pressure of defence crisis, will shake the public confidence in the country's currency. The fear that prices will go up makes them rise, and the rise itself generates further fear. The command over real resources that a given creation of new credits provides dwindles rapidly. Galloping inflation sets in. A unit of currency, as well as in terms of foreign currency dwindles towards nothing. Larger public expenditure in connection with national defence financing, through the method of deficit financing accentuates the upward movement in prices. But, as long as an economy remains far away from the full employment, there is a vast possibility of idle resources to be employed. Needless to say the inflationary method of war finance does not only lead to a rise in the prices of commodities but it also reduces the effective management of defence spending because the government has to spend more to get the same.

The foregoing analysis suggests that though the creation of new money and bank credits may be a convenient means of meeting defence requirements at an early stage, before there has been time to organise an adequate scheme of taxation and public loans, yet the method is inherently bad. It may be pointed out that a government should refrain herself from enjoying over-doses of deficit financing. Thus, the government should restrict war financing through deficit beyond the narrowest possible limits.

In connection with the above analysis, it is worth to point out further the risk involved in relying too heavily, respectively, on expansionist and non-expansionist methods of war finance. If it is assumed that the government borrows heavily from banks, financing by creating much new money, putting it into the money-stream, the following consequences may well be explored:

(1) An expanding stimulus is given to the production of non-defence goods, thereby keeping up non-defence employment.
(2) There seems to be the risk of 'inflation'—a rise, perhaps large, in prices generally.
(3) There is risk of impeding the use and transfer of resources in the production of defence goods, because the demand for non-defence goods is strong.

If contrary to the previous assumption, if the government borrows little or none from banks, and endeavours to divert a large stream of money from the public by taxes or loans; these consequences follow:

1. The demand for non-defence goods is curtailed and unemployment may be caused thereby.

2. The potential inflation is kept under control, i.e. there is no stimulus given toward rising prices.
3. Increased production of defence goods is facilitated because resources find that the demand for their services in non-defence production is going down.

In sum, the choice between these two deviations from perfection depends heavily on one's estimate of the comparative advantages and risks. Now, since the achievement of perfection is not feasible, it can be argued that the government should lean towards overuse of non-expansionist methods of financing war. Hence, heavy reliance should be placed on taxes and public loans and little on bank borrowing and creation of new money, i.e. deficit financing.

**The Empirics**

Research studies on the impact of defence spending on economic growth have often produced inconsistent and conflicting results. Ever since Benoit's (1973) study, a substantial number of researchers have analysed the issue both conceptually and statistically. However, no consensus has emerged. Benoit (1973) studied the relationship between defence spending as a percentage of GNP and the growth rate of civilian GNP in forty-four developing countries for the period from 1950 to 1965 and from 1960 to 1965. After controlling for the effects of foreign investment and bilateral economic aid, his results indicated the presence of a significant cross-country positive correlation between these two variables for the 1960 to 1965 period. In his view, higher defence spending was more likely to be the cause rather than the effect of economic growth. His study initiated a series of books, articles, and papers which tried to replicate, modify, and reanalyze his results.

Kennedy (1974) and Whynes (1979) used Benoit's methodology to show positive cross-national effects of defence spending on economic growth. Studies by Deger and Smith (1983), and Fredericksen and Looney (1983), on the other hand, reported a negative relationship between defence spending and economic growth for at least a majority of the developing countries in their sample. Deger and Smith (1983) argued that military expenditures retard economic development. Deger and

Sen (1983), Leontief and Dutchin (1983), and Faini, Annez, and Taylor (1984) also found evidence to reject the claim that defence spending stimulates economic growth. Smith and Smith (1980) reported the absence of any strong and systematic relationship between these two variables. Similarly, using data for the periods 1960 to 1970 and 1970 to 1977 for a fairly large number of middle income and low income countries, Biswas and Ram (1986) found no consistent, statistically significant relationship between military spending and economic growth.

Several studies reported substantially different trade-offs between these two variables among individual countries. Fredericksen and Looney (1983) used data for a cross-sectional sample of resource-rich and resource-constrained less developed countries (LDCs) for the period 1960 to 1978 and concluded that defence spending helps economic growth in resource-rich LDCs but not in resource-constrained LDCs. Lim (1983) also showed that the negative impacts of defence spending on economic growth were more pronounced among the poorer countries in Africa.

There are several versions of the defence spending-economic growth proposition. First, Benoit (1973, 1978) has shown that defence spending may stimulate growth by increasing aggregate demand. The additional demand generated by higher defence spending leads to increased utilisation of capital stock, lower resource costs, and higher labour employment. The LDCs usually suffer from idle capacity, high unemployment, and underconsumption due to a lack of aggregate demand. Hence, increased utilisation of capital stock may lead to an increase in the profit rate. Increased profits may then lead to higher investment which, in turn, will generate both short-run multiplier effects as well as higher long-term rates of economic growth. In this case, defence spending appears to be causally prior to economic growth.

Moreover, it has also been suggested that defence spending may help economic growth through a spin-off effect (Deger, 1986). In the LDCs, the military is undoubtedly one of the most modern institutions and thus may help in creating a socio-economic structure conductive to growth. The military may engage in research and development, provide technical skills, educational training, and create an infrastructure necessary for economic development. This will have a positive indirect effect on growth. Neuman's (1978) study strongly supports the modernizing influence of the Iranian military program.

On the other hand, defence spending can be detrimental to economic growth in several ways. First, defence expenditures can divert available resources from domestic capital formation, thus reducing potential savings available for investment. This will increase the savings-investment gap and can eventually reduce economic growth. Second, as Deger suggests, "Additional saving . . . will mean not only more capital stock but also better capital stock. If an increased defence burden reduces the amount of new capital formation from the level it could have attained, then the economy suffers from a lowering of both the quantity and quality of its capital stock" (1986, 183).

Third, Rothschild (1977) pointed out the possibility of a round-about effect of defence spending via reduced availabilities of growth products for exports with consequent growth-damping effects. Fourth, the absorption of public expenditure in defence may lead to a shortage of available funds in other fields, for example, education, health, development aid, and so on. Finally, military burdens may also depress growth through the inflationary process they generate.

Krishnamurty and Shome (2008) gives an overview of the analytical and empirical literature on the economics of peace dividend. They opine that disarmament can be viewed as an investment process and the net gain to the economy can be considered as social rate of return. There is no denying the desirability of arms reduction and disarmament. However, it may be argued that in view of increasing militarisation and nuclearisation, the chances of reaping such dividend are bleak.

The mechanisms through which defence spending may influence economic growth are based on the assumption that defence spending is casually prior to economic growth. Most studies in this area make this assumption to estimate their regression of economic growth on defence spending. Some additional variables are also included in these regressions. However, Joerding (1986) showed that no attempt has been made to test the assumption that economic growth is casually prior to defence spending. Although the hypotheses mentioned above imply either a positive or a negative correlation between these two variables, so do other hypotheses with quite different policy implications. Defence spending may lead to changes in economic growth, but it is also plausible that economic growth may cause defence spending. For instance, a country with a high economic growth rate may be willing to strengthen its armed forces through increased defence expenditures. On the other hand, it is theoretically plausible for a country with a high rate of economic growth to divert resources from defence spending to more productive domestic capital formation. Very few of the studies mentioned above have ventured to test this proposition. Hence, augmentation of an inter-disciplinary research on the economics of defence is an academic necessity.

## The Kargil Aftermath

Estimates show that for nearly twenty five years after 1962, the average annual share of defence allocations was around 3 per cent of GDP. An important factor that helped India's defence preparedness during the period was its access to defence equipment from the Soviet sources on soft credit and at prices which were often significantly cheaper than the market prices. By 1987-88, defence expenditure as a proportion of GDP had risen to its highest level of 3.59 per cent. This needs to be seen in the context of the comparatively higher cost of weapons and manpower, the deteriorating security environment following the Soviet intervention in Afghanistan and the massive build up of Pakistan's armed forces.

It is important to observe here that some questions have been raised about the impact of declining defence expenditure on the nation's capacity to counter effectively the Kargil intrusion and, in particular, the preparedness of the jawans for high altitude conflict. However, experiences show that a paucity of resources was not responsible for any lack of preparedness for the Kargil conflict. The prioritisation of threats among external intelligence agency and the Army did not provide for Kargil-type intrusions and consequently their policies in regard to appropriate efforts for space and aerial surveillance as well as reserves to be maintained were influenced by it. The harsh mountain terrain of the Kargil sector was considered virtually impregnable in winter. Nonetheless, when the intrusions were detected, the required clothing, equipment and other stores were provided from reserves; some shortage of special clothing was made up by extreme cold clothing and part worn special (glacial), clothing of troops which had returned from Siachen. However, there was some shortage of sleeping bags and boots. Most items needed for the Kargil War were affordable within the available outlays. Such operational voids as did indeed exist are attributable primarily to procurement procedures and cycle (which includes exploration of indigenous options before imports, finalisation of technical specifications, vendor identification, trials, etc.), prioritisation and the element of surprise in Kargil.

It is surely a matter of serious concern that the brunt of the Kargil War had to be borne out by the foot soldiers. They had to climb high mountains under extreme cold in pitch darkness. They had to carry heavy loads of weapons, ammunition, rations and other requirements which made their task even more arduous. There appears to be an imperative need to give a high priority to properly equipping infantrymen with weapons, equipment and clothing, suitable for the threats they are required to face in the region. Attention needs to be given to reducing the weight of weapons and stores they have to carry.

It has been pointed out by some analysts that declining defence expenditure and its adverse impact on defence modernisation reinforced the Pakistani perception of the Indian defence services being effete and ineffective. This hypothesis has to be viewed along with others, like Pakistan having been prompted in its Kargil mis-adventure by nuclearisation of the sub-continent; its belief that with nuclearisation it has neutralised India's conventional superiority and that excessive preoccupation with counter-insurgency operations had debilitated the Indian Army. While these and other factors have influenced decision-makers in Pakistan, available data clearly reveal that the inadequacy of resources has had an adverse impact on the modernisation of the Indian Armed Forces.

Indian defence spending has shown considerable growth over the last four decades. The first of these two decades were periods of considerable acceleration in the rate at which India was arming itself, although since 1974 that acceleration has been reversed. This reversal in the acceleration of defence spending is attributable to: (i) the so-called conflict resolution with Pakistan; and (ii) the rapid growth in deficit financing and over-all fiscal imbalances. However, Indian defence spending represents an inter-play of domestic and international political and economic constraints and is likely to be influenced in the future by fiscal consideration as much as by security concerns. Thus, the forces for increased defence spending in India are strong.

It may be suggested here that defence mobilisation in India should incorporate three sectors: civilian sector; investment sector and defence sector. In practice, these may be inseparable. However, these are interpenetrated to each other. Moreover, a separation even on paper may keep their objectives distinctive and thereby merit adequate attention. This calls for the greatest coordination and control so as to optimise the total resource base of the nation. In fact, optimisation involves a well planned and efficient use of total resources in such a manner that wastages and over-lappings are avoided for realizing an optimal scale of civilian consumption, investment and defence capability. This being the case, the Government of India should have three budgets instead of two, viz. Revenue Budget, Capital Budget and Defence Budget. There should, therefore, be complete coordination and integration amongst them. Hence, their annual drafting should reflect the proper balance among the civilian, investment and defence needs.

It is of paramount significance to observe here that over the past years actual defence expenditure has been below the amount required by the defence forces to perform efficiently the tasks allotted to them. This has affected the process of modernisation and also created some unacceptable operational voids. In view of growing international tension added to the hostile attitude adopted by India's nighbouring countries, particularly Pakistan, it is incumbent upon the Indian Government to increase the defence spending; and it is not advisable to go in for a sharp reduction in it. Given the country's resource constraints, the scope for enhancing defence outlays is somewhat limited without tightening up fiscal discipline elsewhere. However, it is surely possible to rationalize the expenditure in order to get rid of the non-essential and unproductive portion of it. Hence, the defence services must seek to extract the maximum value from each defence rupee. This will call for some drastic measures like restructuring of the defence forces, improving effectiveness of manpower, retraining and redeployment, dispensing with avoidable and unnecessary expenditure, rigorous prioritisation and focussing resources in areas likely to enhance the effectiveness of the defence forces in meeting the emerging challenges to the country's security. Thus, the research studies on Indian defence economics should focus on a total reform of defence structure, its interface with civil government, defence production and procurement.

## References


Agarwal, A.N. (1966): Economic Mobilisation for National Defence, Bombay, Asia Publishing House.

Agarwal, R. (1978): Defence Production and Development, Arnold-Heinemann, New Delhi.

Ball, N. and Leitenberg, M. (Eds.) (1983): The Structure of Defence Industry. London and Canberra, Croom Helm.

Ball, N. (1988): Security and Economy in the Third World, Princeton, N.J., Princeton University Press.

Benoit, E. (1973): Defence and Economic Growth in Developing Countries. Lexington, M.A., D.C. Health and Co.

Benoit, E. (1978): "Growth and Defence in Developing Counries", *Economic Development and Cultural Change,* No. 26.

Bishwas, B., and R. Ram (1986): "Military Expenditures and Economic Growth in Less-developed Countries: An Augmented Model and Further Evidence", *Economic Development and Cultural Change,* Vol. 34.

Chaudhary, A.R. (1991): "A Causal Analysis of Defence Spending and Economic Growth", *Journal of Conflict Resolution,* Vol. 35, No. 1, March.

Clarke, R.W.B. (1940): Economic Effort of War, London.

Day, A.C.L. (1960): "The Economics of Defence", *Political Quarterly,* Vol. 31, No. 1, January-March.

Cronin, Richard P. (1990): "India's Growing Milittary Might Worry its Neighbours", *Defence Journal,* Vol. 16, No. 6, June.

Deger, S. (1986): "Economic Development and Defence Expenditure", *Economic Development and Cultural Change,* Vol. 34.

Deger, S. (1985): "Human Resources, Government Education Expenditure and the Military Burdens in Less Developed Countries", *The Journal of Developing Areas,* Vol. 20, No. 1.

Deger, S. (1986): Military Expenditure in the Third World: The Economic Effects, London, Routledge and Kegan Paul.

Deger, S., Somnath Sen (1983): "Military Expenditure, Spin-off and Economic Development", *Journal of Development Economics,* Vol. 13.

Deger, S. and R. Smith (1983): "Military Expenditure and Growth in Less-developed Countries, *Journal of Conflict Resolution,* Vol. 27.

Dune, J.P. and R.P. Smith. (1984): "The Economic Copnsequences of Reduced UK Military Expenditure", *Cambridge Journal of Economics*, No. 8.

Dunne, P. (1990): "The Political Economy of Military Expenditure: An Introduction", *Cambridge Journal of Economics*, No. 14.

Faini, R.P., Annez and Taylor. (1984): "Defence Spending, Economic Structure and Growth: Evidence Among Countries over Time", *Economic Development and Cultural Change*, No. 32.

Fontanel, Jacques (1990): "The Economic Effects of Military Expenditure in Third World Countries", *Journal of Peace Research*, Vol. 27, No. 4.

Frederiksen, P.C. and R.E. Looney (1982): "Defence Expenditure and Economic Growth in Developing Countries: Some Further Empirical Evidence", *Journal of Economic Development*, No. 7.

Frederiksen, P.C. and R.E. Looney. (1983): "Defence Expenditure and Economic Growth in Developing Counries", *Armed Forces and Society*, No. 9, Summer.

Frederiksen, P.C. and R.E. Looney (1985), "Another Look at the Defence Spending and Development Hypothesis", *Defence Analysis*, Vol. 1, No. 3.

Frederiksen, P.C. and R.E. Looney (1986): "Defence Expenditure, External Public Debt and Growth in Developing Counries", *Journal of Peace Research*, Vol. 23, No. 1.

Gandhi, Ved P. (1974): "India's Self-Inflicted Defence Burden", *EPW*, Aug 31.

Ghosh, A.K. (1996): India's Defence Budget and Expenditure Management in a Wider Context, Lancer Publishers, New Delhi.

Government of India (2000): From Surprise to Reckoning, The Kargil Review Committee Report, New Delhi.

Grober L.M. and R.C. Porter (1989): "Benoit Revisited: Defence Spending and Economic Growth in LDCs", *Journal of Conflict Resolution*, Vol. 33.

Grant, Brig. N.B. (Retd.) (1989): "Defence Budget and National Security", *Combat Journal*, Vol. 16, No. 3, December.

Hirst, F.W. (1911): "The Policy and Finance of Modern Armaments", paper read to the Manchester Statistical Society, 13, December, preface, page v.

Hirst, F.W. (1916): The Political Economy of War, London, p. 3.

Hirst, F.W. (1934): The Consequences of the War to Great Britain, Oxford.

Hitch, C.J. and Roland McKean (1973): The Economics of Defence in the Nuclear Age, New York, Athene.

Joerding, W. (1986): "Economic Growth and Defence Spending: Granger Casuality", *Journal of Development Economics*, No. 21, April.

Jung, W.S. and P.J. Marshall. (1985): "Exports Growth and Casuality in Developing Countries", *Journal of Development Economics*, No. 18.

Kalam, A. (1990): "Defence Production in the Third World", *Defence Journal*, Vol. 16, No. 3, March.

Katoch, G.C. (1992): "Defence Expenditure: Some Issues", *Indian Defence Review*, January.

Krishnamurty, K. and Samik Shome (2008): "Economics of Arms Reduction and Peace Dividend: A Survey", *The Indian Economic Journal*, Vol. 56, No. 1, April-June.

Leontief, W. and Faye Duchin. (1983): Milittary Spending: Facts and Figures, Worldwide Implications and Future Outlook. New York, Oxford University Press.

Lim, David (1983): "Another Look at Growth and Defence in Less Developed Countries", *Economic Development and Cultural Change*, No. 31.

Looney, R.E. (1987): "Determinants of Military Expenditures in Developing Countries", *The Journal of Arms Control and Disarmament*, Vol. 8, No. 3.

Matthews, R.G. (1989): "The Development of India's Defence Industrial Base", *Journal of Strategic Studies*, Voi. 12, No. 4, December.

Pigon, A.C. (1921): Political Economy of War, London.

Rothschild, K.W. (1970): "Military Expenditure, Exports and Growth", *Kyklos*, Vol. 30.

Schultze, C.L. (1981): "Economic Effects of Defence Budget", *Bookings Bulletin*, 18 (2).

Singh, Jasjit (1992): "Trends in Defence Expenditure", *Asian Strategic Review*, 1991-92. New Delhi, IDSA.

SIPRI. World Armaments and Disarmament Yearbook (Annual Reports).

Subrahamanyam, K. (1973): Defence and Development, Calcutta, Minerva.

Tiwari, AP (1991): "A Macro Economic Model of Defence Market", in Conference Volume, Indian Economic Association, 74th Conference, Anantpur.

Tiwari, A.P. (1993) "A Non-market Theory of Optiimum Defence Output: Some Reflections", in Debendra K. Das (ed), Economics of Markets: Theory and Evidence, Deep and Deep.

Tiwari, A.P. (1993): "Structure and Burden of Defence Expenditure", in Sengupta A.K. (ed) Union Budget '93: Issues and Implications.

Tiwari, A.P. (2006): The Fiscal Impact of Defence Mobilisation in India, 1962-72; unpublished doctoral dissertation, University of Lucknow, Lucknow.

Whynes. David K. (1979): The Economics of Third World Milittary Expenditure, University of Texas press.

Word, M.D. and A.K. Mahajan (1984): "Defence Expenditures, Security Threats, and Governmental Deficits", *Journal of Conflict Resolution*, Vol. 28, No. 3.

Weede, E. (1983): "Military Participation Ratios, Human Capital Formation and Economic Growth: A Cross National Analysis", *Journal of Political and Military Sociology*, 11 (Spring).

# Index